TENNYSON AND BROWNING

ALFRED TENNYSON
AS A YOUNG MAN

*From a pen-drawing by
E. Heber Thompson*

TENNYSON AND BROWNING

Contrasted
by
GUY BOAS

THOMAS NELSON & SONS, Ltd.
LONDON, EDINBURGH, AND NEW YORK

First Edition published May 1925.
Reprinted November 1925 ; January 1929 ; May 1930 ;
March 1931 ; June 1933 ; February 1934

CONTENTS

PART IV

PART V

ROBERT BROWNING
AS A YOUNG MAN

From a pen-drawing by
E. Heber Thompson

ROBERT BROWNING
AT A YOUNG MAN

INTRODUCTION

To put a tiger-lily and a rose into the same vase does not make harmony, but it arrests attention. Those who have hitherto taken for granted the peculiar beauty of each flower, fall to wondering why, side by side, they do not agree : and as they ponder, they are compelled to consider their separate loveliness afresh.

In the following pages some poems of Tennyson and Browning are put into one volume with the idea of producing a similar result. To draw the two poets into any real unity would be impossible. They did not write to be compared ; they did not even write to be contrasted. Like the flowers, they grew independently, and had nothing in common but the soil.

It would be odd if it were otherwise. A great literary figure raises himself above his fellows just because he is not as they are. He has something to say which has not occurred to them, and a power of saying it which they do not share. In addition to rising above the many, he stands distinct among his peers. It is a law of art that no perfect thing can be repeated. *Corinna goes a-Maying* is no more like *Epithalamion* than it is like *The Rape of the Lock*: all that the three poems share is perfection. So Tennyson's greatness as a master of verbal music is more like the greatness of Browning, the master of psychology, than any similarities which can be traced among the details of their work.

To say that they were both great English poets of the same generation is sufficient comparison. To contrast them is a more intricate and profitable task.

Queen Victoria came to the throne in 1837, to preside over as individual a reign as English history can show. By those who do not like discipline, Victorianism has been turned into a word of reproach : yet, taken for all in all, the word stands for something far wider and more significant. The reign had opened in comparative despondency. The extravagant expectations of reaching in a leap the millennium of universal freedom, current at the beginning of the century, had ended in a long and frantic struggle to save Europe from the tyranny of one man. The share of England in the battle with Napoleon had strained both her coffers and her nerves. As usual the lion had woken late and conquered, but, as now, he was weary with fighting, and wanted to recuperate. Neither the dissolute court of George IV. nor the eccentricities of William IV. had made for repose. But the simple, earnest, responsible girl, who succeeded her uncles, came like a soothing nurse into the national sick-room, and the patient again took life. The example of industry, discipline, and high purpose which for the next sixty years was set by the court bore abundant fruit in due season. At the Diamond Jubilee of the venerable Queen, her colonial and coloured subjects had turned from thousands into millions, trade had increased out of recognition, the land was threaded with railways, sailing ships had turned into ironclads, Reform Bills and Factory Acts, Mines Acts and Trades Unions had brought protection and power to the people. The Tractarian Movement and the heresies of Darwin had revitalized the Church.

PATRIOTIC POEMS

Into every phase of this national progress Tennyson entered, to celebrate and to report. If Victoria was the sick-nurse, the Laureate framed the bulletins. The death of the victor of Waterloo, the battle of Balaclava, the defence of Lucknow, the tragedy of Khartoum, these inspired the Laureate's pen. Is England in danger of French invasion? Is her navy at adequate strength? Have sufficient riflemen formed? Such questions perplex the official Muse, already weighted with official duties. The Opening of the International Exhibition must be sung; a welcome extended to Alexandrovna, Duchess of Edinburgh; the Queen must be sustained in her loss of the Prince Consort.

Never did a Laureate labour more conscientiously or more successfully to interpret the practice and spirit of his age. Born into the typical country rectory, and nurtured in the seclusion of Somersby, Tennyson seems to have absorbed in boyhood the very spirit of England from quiet contact with the Lincolnshire soil that in manhood he might personify her voice.

With Browning it was otherwise. Born into England, he was not of it, and in later life he was rarely in it. While Tennyson was the son of a vicar, Browning's father was a dissenter, which excluded the poet from the public schools and Universities. Consequently when Tennyson had ventured no farther than Cambridge, Browning was already roaming the interior of Russia. While Tennyson was scarcely ever out of England, Browning made Italy a second home. The Laureate was never long sundered from " London's central roar " by more distant waters than the Solent : Browning's " home-thoughts " have invariably to be forwarded " from abroad." To Browning love of country was less than love of men. In his sympathies and interests he was cosmopolitan rather than patriotic. Moreover, Englishmen in many respects were least calculated to engage his attention. Never was Browning happier than when dissecting a crank, a lunatic, a charlatan, a criminal; some odd, abnormal freak. The average Englishman is not odd, and therefore he appealed the less to Browning.

POEMS OF LOVE

In King Arthur of the *Idylls*, Tennyson portrayed
the simple, honourable beauty of conjugal fidelity :

> To love one maiden only, cleave to her,
> And worship her by years of noble deeds.

Though Browning practised this doctrine in his personal life, it was not the aspect of love on which his
literary imagination often dwelt. He preferred to
wander down complicated and sombre by-paths ; to
spy out the fatal wooing of Porphyria ; to overhear
how " all smiles " of " my last Duchess " " stopped
together " ; to prompt Count Guido Franceschini in the
dock. From any one of these persons Tennyson would
have recoiled in horror : each did what no English
gentleman would do. Neither does Browning approve
of villains : but he does not recoil from their presence
until he has probed their condition of mind to the
depths, and helped them to put their hopeless and
shameless cases before the world with the utmost
ability.

Tennyson has his faithless lovers too, but they are
not monsters. Lancelot is false, but he is not a
villain. He does what an English gentleman shouldn't :
Count Guido does what an English gentleman
couldn't.

Love, in Tennyson, is the master-wave which seizes
the young man in the spring, and sweeps him straight
to glory or dishonour. In Browning there are also
the eddies and whirlpools to be explored. As far as
his own life is concerned, *One Word More* washes
straight to glory, but that is not enough to explain the
cross-currents in the tragedy of Andrea, or James Lee ;
to fathom such mysteries he toils unceasingly, con-
templates love *Among the Ruins*, sends lovers out on

a *Last Ride Together*, and watches the mysterious effect of Pippa passing.

Even when, in some short lyric, love is reduced to its simplest terms, and a lady is straightforwardly adored, the voice of each poet is distinct :

> Queen rose of the rosebud garden of girls,
>   Come hither, the dances are done,
> In gloss of satin and glimmer of pearls,
>   Queen lily and rose in one ;
> Shine out, little head, sunning over with curls,
>   To the flowers, and be their sun.

The appeal is as direct as language can make it. The matchless ease of the vowel-play works a melody divinely simple.

> Nay but you, who do not love her,
>   Is she not pure gold, my mistress ?
> Holds earth aught—speak truth—above her ?
>   Aught like this tress, see, and this tress,
> And this last fairest tress of all,
> So fair, see, ere I let it fall ?

Browning, calling this merely *Song*, seems for once determined to put music before everything. Yet complications will creep in : the very agility of the rhyming—" mistress, this tress "—calls attention from the poet's rapture to the poet's brain. Nor can the attitude of the lover's mind which is expounded in the subsequent verse be considered simple : he cannot praise his lady because he loves her too much : he must leave the praising to those who do not. It is fortunate that the wooer of Maud escaped this involved position : had he too been struck dumb in proportion to the intensity of his admiration, the literature of love would have lost eleven of its most lucid and most lovely stanzas.

Tennyson's ideal of love is suggested by his title

Love and Duty. In that poem two lovers cannot marry because duty comes between their embraces. Are their lives therefore wasted ? The answer emphatically is No. Exalted by renunciation, assured of the higher love, the man may live as happily and usefully wedded to the " stern daughter of the voice of God." So too the woman, assured that all " Life needs for life is possible to will," shall tend her flowers contentedly, and if " his " vision should cross her dreams, it shall be only " to point (her) forward to a distant light."

Such reverence for the sanctity of marriage flames like a gospel through all that Tennyson wrote : *Love and Duty* would equally well serve as title for *The Princess* or for the *Idylls*.

The doctrine of love preached by Browning in such a poem as *The Statue and the Bust* is in startling contrast. Duke Ferdinand of Florence desires the young bride of the head of the noble Riccardi house. Daily he rides past the Riccardi palace and sees the lady at her window. The bride returns his admiration, and is confined for ever to her chamber by her suspicious husband. The two lovers are on the point of eloping, but cannot bring themselves to the plunge. For years they exchange distant glances, until they find that age is creeping upon them. Then the lady calls for a sculptor to perpetuate her fading beauty in a bust that shall look for ever from her window ; while the Duke engages another sculptor to fashion him in marble on his horse, and sets the statue in the square to be admired of the bust for ever. The poet reflects on the picture of the lovers when they come to the trump of doom. Then must they realize that in drawing back from one another their object in life was lost :

I hear you reproach, " But delay was best,
For their end was a crime." Oh, a crime will do
As well, I reply, to serve for a test,

> As a virtue golden through and through,
> Sufficient to vindicate itself
> And prove its worth at a moment's view !

Such philosophy, applied relentlessly, would seem to go far to justify the demeanour of Lancelot. But in *The Statue and the Bust* it receives more extreme expression than elsewhere in Browning, and even here it is rather propounded as a theory than recommended as a practice. The real moral of the poem, and one which Browning never tires in urging, is that in affairs of the heart genuine affection must not be sacrificed to expediency. With his own passionate energy Browning could never forgive the sin of the unlit lamp and the ungirt loin.

The same moral is drawn less dangerously in *Youth and Art*, where a young artist and a young singer fail to marry because in the morning of life they lacked funds :

> Each life's unfulfilled, you see,
>   It hangs still, patchy and scrappy :
> We have not sighed deep, laughed free,
>   Starved, feasted, despaired,—been happy.

Such admonition is a long step from *Love and Duty*, and in perplexity the reader may well wonder which voice he shall approve.

It is as easy from the depths of an armchair to welcome the energetic romance of Browning's ideal as to urge that Hamlet should have swept to an instant revenge. The critic, when he has himself to take the leap, is apt to favour less precipitate action. Moreover, though the ideal of Tennyson may make less exciting reading, it is likely to make more happy practice. Even worldly prudence is not always ill-advised : and where a " crime " is involved, the ideal of King Arthur is a possible path to felicity, and a certain path to salvation.

Poems of Art

In his attitude to Art as to Love, the word duty weighs heavily with Tennyson. The matter is discussed with great seriousness in *The Palace of Art*. A soul in love with beauty confines herself in a palace bejewelled with every aesthetic decoration that the mind can picture. Glorious scenery, magnificent architecture, superb paintings, cunning mosaics, chiming bells and radiant lights : all contribute to lull the soul to eternal satisfaction, far from the madding crowd and the troubles of humanity.

> I take possession of man's mind and deed,
> 　　I care not what the sects may brawl.
> I sit as God, holding no form of creed,
> 　　But contemplating all.

Yet the soul grows restless in this lovely isolation. It has courted beauty only for beauty's sake, and has shut itself off from love. Uncertain and terrifying shapes appear in dark corners of the palace, stagnation and paralysis seize the luxurious inmate.

> And death and life she hated equally,
> 　　And nothing saw, for her despair,
> But dreadful time, dreadful eternity,
> 　　No comfort anywhere.

Suddenly she realizes that beauty was never meant to be hugged in a corner as a selfish privilege : it is the child of human love, and where there is no love beauty will die.

> So when four years were wholly finished,
> 　　She threw her royal robes away.
> " Make me a cottage in the vale," she said,
> 　　" Where I may mourn and pray."

The poem effectively chastens those who are demoral-
ized by foolish interpretations of the theory of art for
art's sake. It is less effective in the many cases, of
which Browning's is one, where the problem does not
arise. The poem presents the temptation which besets
the fastidious, and suggests that Tennyson had to
brace himself before entering the lowly domiciles of
The May Queen, or *The Miller's Daughter*.

> O God-like isolation which art mine,
>   I can but count thee perfect gain,
> What time I watch the darkening droves of swine
>   That range on yonder plain.

So mused the tenant of the Palace of Art. Had Browning taken on the lease, he would probably have called
the swine into the drawing-room to keep him company, and composed a blank verse apology for those
who soiled or upset the furniture. He would have
egged them on to drink the flood of fountain-foam,
and prodded them to hear their grunts contrasted with
the " low preamble " of the nightingale.

But never in the first place can one imagine Browning tempted into such isolation. Rather than shutting
themselves off from the world, his artists are in danger
of falling too deliriously in love with it.

So far from enjoying the seclusion of the Palace of
Medici, Fra Lippo must let himself down from the
windows to have a night's frolic with the girls. It is
the tragedy of Andrea that into his visions of eternal
beauty the mundane smile of Lucretia will always
break. Browning had too much humour to be fastidious : his artists love all life, high or low. They
have inherited the Catholic outlook inspired by the
Picture at Fano. Fra Lippo embraces it : Andrea
mourns that he has not lived up to it :

> O world, as God has made it ! All is beauty :
>   And knowing this, is love, and love is duty.
> What further may be sought for or declared ?

The conflict in *The Palace of Art* was between Love and Beauty, as in another of Tennyson's poems between Love and Duty. Instinctively to Browning and to Browning's artists, Love is Beauty—Love is Duty.

POEMS OF FAITH

Though usually it is Tennyson who is simple, and Browning curious, in the matter of faith the position is reversed. However tortuously Browning at times expresses it, his creed is simple and unchanging :

> Grow old along with me !
> The best is yet to be,
> The last of life, for which the first was made :
> Our times are in His hand
> Who saith, " A whole I planned,
> Youth shows but half ; trust God : see all, nor be afraid."

The optimism of Rabbi Ben Ezra is that of Browning himself ; and he bequeaths it to many speakers. " Have you found your life distasteful ? " asks Browning's Shakespeare at the Mermaid, " My life did and does smack sweet." " God's in His Heaven, all's right with the world," carols Pippa. " On the earth the broken arcs, in the Heaven a perfect round," echoes Abt Vogler. Such sentiments are not dramatic, but the personal persuasion of the author, who held as tenaciously at the close of his own life as at the start that " we fall to rise, are baffled to fight better, sleep to wake." Life in Browning is an adventure, in which, considering the odds against him, a man cannot help giving a good account of himself provided only that he does not shirk the issue or throw up the fight. Let years of activity bring their inevitable quota of experience, and at the time when the body is coming to the end of its strength, the soul is sufficiently proved to enter into that state of perfection which is Heaven. Such optimism has found cynical critics, who count it the result of a good digestion. But even if they could prove Browning an automatic optimist, they could not prove him a superficial one. No believer has ever entered more sympathetically into the position of the agnostic, nor set his flowers among a more deliberate cluster of thorns. It might not have taken an intricate mind to fashion the faith of Pippa or Pompilia, but it was no unsophisticated or sheltered vision that peered into the dark backgrounds of Sebald and Guido against which the light is broken.

To a like measure of certainty Tennyson never attained. In the engagement of *The Two Voices*, the Voice of Faith wins on points, but there is no knock-out blow. King Arthur, after a life of perfect Christian sentiment and practice, enters nothing more celestial than a vague Valhalla with a prospect of good weather. The poet himself does no more than " hope " to see his Pilot, after crossing the bar.

Browning's faith stands like an immovable headland, against which the poet himself sets the storms of doubt in motion that he may smile serenely at the waters which break themselves in vain. Tennyson's faith is as an artificial breakwater, which has much power of resistance, yet is in constant need of human strengthening.

Rabbi Ben Ezra argues his case, not for his own need, but for those who do not share his conviction. Tennyson must always address himself. It is significant that always in his premises he reasons, and for conclusion falls back on intuition and emotion, whereas in Browning intellect serves faith as surely as doubt. The case for suicide is put by the dark Voice as a logical proposition :

> Thou art so full of misery
> Were it not better not to be ?

The answer is one of sentiment :

> To feel, altho' no tongue can prove,
> That every cloud, that spreads above
> And veileth love, itself is love.

On such reasoning the whole negative side of *In Memoriam* is built, and with such emotion the positive. Never once is the intellectual positive of Bishop Blougram brought into play :

> All we have gained then by our unbelief
> Is a life of doubt diversified by faith,
> For one of faith diversified by doubt :
> We called the chess-board white,—we call it black.

That Tennyson's message of faith should be less certain than Browning's is not the necessary consequence of his reliance on an emotional positive. There are many reasons for trusting intuition rather than logic in such matters ; as Blougram himself suggests by the " sudden sunset touch."

The greater uncertainty of Tennyson is apparent not in his method, but in result. His emotional answers do not seem to satisfy himself. The loss of Arthur Hallam plunges him into an almost panic-stricken grief, to which one by one the stanzas of *In Memoriam* bring support and comfort. But do they bring assurance ?—that pulsing, invincible assurance that shows the author of *Prospice* straining at the leash to be let loose on the adventure of Death, knowing that it means only a triumphant leap into the arms of his beloved.

It is a common and superficial criticism of Tennyson that he is confined in the narrow outlook of a Victorian rectory. But had the poet followed in his father's footsteps, his poems translated into sermons would have puzzled the simple faith of the Somersby parishioners, and it is to be doubted whether the

Laureate would ever have entered the House of Lords by way of the Episcopal Bench.

On the other hand it is a tribute to the complexity of human nature that from Browning, the artist, the *bon vivant*, the social virtuoso, the criminologist, the psycho-analyst, the man-about-town, about-Europe, about-the-world, there shines a faith as simple as Pippa's and as influential.

TENNYSON AS LYRIC STYLIST: BROWNING AS DRAMATIC REALIST

But in the last place, a poet will be judged as a poet, and not as a philosopher, or preacher, or psychologist. That which finally holds Tennyson and Browning apart is a quality which cannot be put as a one-word heading over a section of poems. Tennyson at his finest is one of the world's greatest masters of ornate verbal music—the music of Virgil and Milton. Browning at his best approaches Shakespeare in his sense of the dramatic, his subtlety, and his power of tense and vivid description.

English literature has nothing else to show like *My Last Duchess*, or *Porphyria's Lover*, or *The Grammarian's Funeral*, and by such creations Browning's immortality may ultimately prove to be most assured.

Browning wrote lyrics of beauty, but the lyrics of Tennyson are more beautiful: his blank verse is noble, yet it falls below Shakespeare. But the curious grave of the Grammarian is alone upon the mountains, and can be compared or contrasted neither with the work of Tennyson nor any other.

The summit of Tennyson is neither curious nor lonely. It is a matchless dignity of music, simple in effect if not in making. Other poets have equalled his musicianship, but not Browning. Nothing like the exquisite melody of the *Lady of Shalott*, *Œnone*, or *The Lotos-Eaters*, is to be heard in Browning. To this sheer music of Tennyson men will listen long after they have discounted his theories and discarded his philosophy.

The end is as the beginning. The more the tiger-lily and the rose are scrutinized the more unlike they appear in all respects but one : both, at their freshest, are perfection.

G. B.

TENNYSON AND BROWNING

PART I

TENNYSON AS LYRIC STYLIST : BROWNING AS DRAMATIC REALIST

"HOW THEY BROUGHT THE GOOD NEWS FROM GHENT TO AIX"

I SPRANG to the stirrup, and Joris, and he ;
I galloped, Dirck galloped, we galloped all three ;
"Good speed ! " cried the watch, as the gate-bolts
    undrew ;
"Speed ! " echoed the wall to us galloping through ;
Behind shut the postern, the lights sank to rest,
And into the midnight we galloped abreast.

Not a word to each other ; we kept the great pace
Neck by neck, stride by stride, never changing our
    place ;
I turned in my saddle and made its girths tight,
Then shortened each stirrup, and set the pique right,
Rebuckled the cheek-strap, chained slacker the bit,
Nor galloped less steadily Roland a whit.

'Twas moonset at starting ; but while we drew near
Lokeren, the cocks crew and twilight dawned clear ;
At Boom, a great yellow star came out to see ;
At Düffeld, 'twas morning as plain as could be ;
And from Mecheln church-steeple we heard the half-
    chime,
So, Joris broke silence with, " Yet there is time ! "

At Aershot, up leaped of a sudden the sun,
And against him the cattle stood black every one,
To stare thro' the mist at us galloping past,
And I saw my stout galloper Roland at last,
With resolute shoulders, each butting away
The haze, as some bluff river headland its spray :

And his low head and crest, just one sharp ear bent
    back
For my voice, and the other pricked out on his track ;
And one eye's black intelligence,—ever that glance
O'er its white edge at me, his own master, askance !
And the thick heavy spume-flakes which aye and anon
His fierce lips shook upwards in galloping on.

By Hasselt, Dirck groaned ; and cried Joris, " Stay
    spur !
Your Roos galloped bravely, the fault's not in her,
We'll remember at Aix "—for one heard the quick
    wheeze
Of her chest, saw the stretched neck and staggering
    knees,
And sunk tail, and horrible heave of the flank,
As down on her haunches she shuddered and sank.

So, we were left galloping, Joris and I,
Past Looz and past Tongres, no cloud in the sky ;
The broad sun above laughed a pitiless laugh,
'Neath our feet broke the brittle bright stubble like
    chaff ;

Till over by Dalhem a dome-spire sprang white,
And " Gallop," gasped Joris, " for Aix is in sight ! "

" How they'll greet us ! "—and all in a moment his
   roan
Rolled neck and croup over, lay dead as a stone ;
And there was my Roland to bear the whole weight
Of the news which alone could save Aix from her fate,
With his nostrils like pits full of blood to the brim,
And with circles of red for his eye-sockets' rim.

Then I cast loose my buffcoat, each holster let fall,
Shook off both my jack-boots, let go belt and all,
Stood up in the stirrup, leaned, patted his ear,
Called my Roland his pet-name, my horse without
   peer ;
Clapped my hands, laughed and sang, any noise, bad
   or good,
Till at length into Aix Roland galloped and stood.

And all I remember is, friends flocking round
As I sat with his head 'twixt my knees on the ground ;
And no voice but was praising this Roland of mine,
As I poured down his throat our last measure of wine,
Which (the burgesses voted by common consent)
Was no more than his due who brought good news
   from Ghent.

                              ROBERT BROWNING.

BEFORE

I

LET them fight it out, friend ! things have gone too far.
God must judge the couple : leave them as they are
—Whichever one's the guiltless, to his glory,
And whichever one the guilt's with, to my story !

II

Why, you would not bid men, sunk in such a slough,
Strike no arm out further, stick and stink as now,
Leaving right and wrong to settle the embroilment,
Heaven with snaky hell, in torture and entoilment?

III

Who's the culprit of them? How must he conceive
God—the queen he caps to, laughing in his sleeve,
" 'Tis but decent to profess oneself beneath her :
Still, one must not be too much in earnest, either ! "

IV

Better sin the whole sin, sure that God observes ;
Then go live his life out ! Life will try his nerves,
When the sky, which noticed all, makes no disclosure,
And the earth keeps up her terrible composure.

V

Let him pace at pleasure, past the walls of rose,
Pluck their fruits when grape-trees graze him as he
goes !
For he 'gins to guess the purpose of the garden,
With the sly mute thing, beside there, for a warden.

VI

What's the leopard-dog-thing, constant at his side,
A leer and lie in every eye of its obsequious hide ?
When will come an end to all the mock obeisance,
And the price appear that pays for the misfeasance ?

VII

So much for the culprit. Who's the martyred man ?
Let him bear one stroke more, for be sure he can !
He that strove thus evil's lump with good to leaven,
Let him give his blood at last and get his heaven !

VIII

All or nothing, stake it ! Trusts he God or no ?
Thus far and no farther ? farther ? be it so !
Now, enough of your chicane of prudent pauses,
Sage provisos, sub-intents and saving-clauses !

IX

Ah, " forgive," you bid him ?   While God's champion
  lives,
Wrong shall be resisted : dead, why, he forgives,
But you must not end my friend ere you begin him ;
Evil stands not crowned on earth, while breath is in
  him.

X

Once more—Will the wronger, at this last of all,
Dare to say, " I did wrong," rising in his fall ?
No ?—Let go, then ! Both the fighters to their places !
While I count three, step you back as many paces !

ROBERT BROWNING.

AFTER

TAKE the cloak from his face, and at first
  Let the corpse do its worst !

How he lies in his rights of a man !
  Death has done all death can.
And, absorbed in the new life he leads,
  He recks not, he heeds
Nor his wrong nor my vengeance ; both strike
  On his senses alike,
And are lost in the solemn and strange
  Surprise of the change.

Ha, what avails death to erase
  His offence, my disgrace ?

I would we were boys as of old
  In the field, by the fold :
His outrage, God's patience, man's scorn
  Were so easily borne !

I stand here now, he lies in his place :
  Cover the face !

ROBERT BROWNING.

MEMORABILIA

Ah, did you once see Shelley plain,
  And did he stop and speak to you,
And did you speak to him again ?
  How strange it seems and new !

But you were living before that,
  And also you are living after ;
And the memory I started at—
  My starting moves your laughter !

I crossed a moor, with a name of its own
  And a certain use in the world no doubt,
Yet a hand's-breadth of it shines alone
  Mid the blank miles round about :

For there I picked up on the heather
  And there I put inside my breast
A moulted feather, an eagle-feather !
  Well, I forget the rest.

ROBERT BROWNING.

MY LAST DUCHESS

FERRARA

That's my last Duchess painted on the wall,
Looking as if she were alive. I call

That piece a wonder, now : Frà Pandolf's hands
Worked busily a day, and there she stands.
Will't please you sit and look at her ?   I said
" Frà Pandolf " by design, for never read
Strangers like you that pictured countenance,
The depth and passion of its earnest glance,
But to myself they turned (since none puts by
The curtain I have drawn for you, but I)
And seemed as they would ask me, if they durst,
How such a glance came there ;   so, not the first
Are you to turn and ask thus. Sir, 'twas not
Her husband's presence only, called that spot
Of joy into the Duchess' cheek :   perhaps
Frà Pandolf chanced to say " Her mantle laps
Over my lady's wrist too much," or " Paint
Must never hope to reproduce the faint
Half-flush that dies along her throat : " such stuff
Was courtesy, she thought, and cause enough
For calling up that spot of joy.   She had
A heart—how shall I say ?—too soon made glad,
Too easily impressed ;   she liked whate'er
She looked on, and her looks went everywhere.
Sir, 'twas all one ! My favour at her breast,
The dropping of the daylight in the West,
The bough of cherries some officious fool
Broke in the orchard for her, the white mule
She rode with round the terrace—all and each
Would draw from her alike the approving speech,
Or blush, at least.   She thanked men,—good ! but
     thanked
Somehow—I know not how—as if she ranked
My gift of a nine-hundred-years-old name
With anybody's gift.   Who'd stoop to blame
This sort of trifling ?   Even had you skill
In speech—(which I have not)—to make your will
Quite clear to such an one, and say, " Just this
Or that in you disgusts me ;   here you miss,
Or there exceed the mark "—and if she let

Herself be lessoned so, nor plainly set
Her wits to yours, forsooth, and made excuse,
—E'en then would be some stooping ; and I choose
Never to stoop. Oh sir, she smiled, no doubt,
Whene'er I passed her ; but who passed without
Much the same smile ?   This grew ; I gave commands ;
Then all smiles stopped together.   There she stands
As if alive. Will't please you rise ? We'll meet
The company below, then. I repeat,
The Count your master's known munificence
Is ample warrant that no just pretence
Of mine for dowry will be disallowed ;
Though his fair daughter's self, as I avowed
At starting, is my object. Nay, we'll go
Together down, sir. Notice Neptune, though,
Taming a sea-horse, thought a rarity,
Which Claus of Innsbruck cast in bronze for me !

ROBERT BROWNING.

INSTANS TYRANNUS

Of the million or two, more or less,
  I rule and possess,
One man, for some cause undefined,
  Was least to my mind.

I struck him, he grovelled of course—
  For, what was his force ?
I pinned him to earth with my weight
And persistence of hate :
And he lay, would not moan, would not curse,
  As his lot might be worse.

" Were the object less mean, would he stand
  At the swing of my hand !
For obscurity helps him and blots
  The hole where he squats."

So, I set my five wits on the stretch
To inveigle the wretch.
All in vain ! Gold and jewels I threw,
Still he couched there perdue ;
I tempted his blood and his flesh,
Hid in roses my mesh,
Choicest cates and the flagon's best spilth :
Still he kept to his filth.

Had he kith now or kin, were access
To his heart, did I press—
Just a son or a mother to seize !
No such booty as these.
Were it simply a friend to pursue
'Mid my million or two,
Who could pay me in person or pelf
What he owes me himself !
No : I could not but smile through my chafe :
For the fellow lay safe
As his mates do, the midge and the nit,
—Through minuteness, to wit.

Then a humour more great took its place
At the thought of his face,
The droop, the low cares of the mouth,
The trouble uncouth
'Twixt the brows, all that air one is fain
To put out of its pain.
And, " no ! " I admonished myself,
" Is one mocked by an elf,
Is one baffled by toad or by rat ?
The gravamen's in that !
How the lion, who crouches to suit
His back to my foot,
Would admire that I stand in debate !
But the small turns the great
If it vexes you,—that is the thing !
Toad or rat vex the king ?

Though I waste half my realm to unearth
Toad or rat, 'tis well worth ! "

So, I soberly laid my last plan
To extinguish the man.
Round his creep-hole, with never a break
Ran my fires for his sake ;
Over-head, did my thunder combine
With my under-ground mine :
Till I looked from my labour content
To enjoy the event.

When sudden . . . how think ye, the end ?
Did I say " without friend ? "
Say rather, from marge to blue marge
The whole sky grew his targe
With the sun's self for visible boss,
While an Arm ran across
Which the earth heaved beneath like a breast
Where the wretch was safe prest !
Do you see ?   Just my vengeance complete,
The man sprang to his feet,
Stood erect, caught at God's skirts, and prayed !
—So, I was afraid !

ROBERT BROWNING.

✕ PORPHYRIA'S LOVER

THE rain set early in to-night,
　　The sullen wind was soon awake,
It tore the elm-tops down for spite,
　　And did its worst to vex the lake,
　　I listened with heart fit to break.
When glided in Porphyria ; straight
　　She shut the cold out and the storm,
And kneeled and made the cheerless grate
　　Blaze up, and all the cottage warm ;

When done, she rose, and from her form
Withdrew the dripping cloak and shawl,
   And laid her soiled gloves by, untied
Her hat and let the damp hair fall,
   And, last, she sat down by my side
   And called me. When no voice replied
She put my arm about her waist,
   And made her smooth white shoulder bare,
And all her yellow hair displaced,
   And, stooping, made my cheek lie there,
   And spread o'er all her yellow hair,
Murmuring how she loved me—she
   Too weak, for all her heart's endeavour,
To set its struggling passions free
   From pride, and vainer ties dissever,
   And give herself to me for ever.
But passion sometimes would prevail,
   Nor could to-night's gay feast restrain
A sudden thought of one so pale
   For love of her, and all in vain :
   So, she was come through wind and rain.
Be sure I looked up at her eyes
   Happy and proud ; at last I knew
Porphyria worshipped me ; surprise
   Made my heart swell, and still it grew
   While I debated what to do.
That moment she was mine, mine, fair,
   Perfectly pure and good ; I found
A thing to do, and all her hair
   In one long yellow string I wound
   Three times her little throat around
And strangled her. No pain felt she ;
   I am quite sure she felt no pain :
As a shut bud that holds a bee,
   I warily oped her lids ; again
   Laughed the blue eyes without a stain.
And I untightened next the tress
   About her neck ; her cheek once more

Blushed bright beneath my burning kiss :
  I propped her head up as before,
  Only, this time *my* shoulder bore
Her head, which droops upon it still :
  The smiling rosy little head,
So glad it has its utmost will,
  That all it scorned at once is fled,
  And I, its love, am gained instead !
Porphyria's love : she guessed not how
  Her darling one wish would be heard.
And thus we sit together now,
  And all night long we have not stirred,
  And yet God has not said a word !

ROBERT BROWNING.

INCIDENT OF THE FRENCH CAMP

You know, we French stormed Ratisbon :
  A mile or so away
On a little mound, Napoleon
  Stood on our storming-day ;
With neck out-thrust, you fancy how,
  Legs wide, arms locked behind,
As if to balance the prone brow
  Oppressive with its mind.

Just as perhaps he mused " My plans
  That soar, to earth may fall,
Let once my army-leader Lannes
  Waver at yonder wall,"—
Out 'twixt the battery-smokes there flew
  A rider, bound on bound
Full-galloping ; nor bridle drew
  Until he reached the mound.

Then off there flung in smiling joy,
  And held himself erect

By just his horse's mane, a boy :
   You hardly could suspect—
(So tight he kept his lips compressed,
   Scarce any blood came through)
You looked twice ere you saw his breast
   Was all but shot in two.

' Well," cried he, " Emperor, by God's grace
   We've got you Ratisbon !
The Marshal's in the market-place,
   And you'll be there anon
To see your flag-bird flap his vans
   Where I, to heart's desire,
Perched him ! "   The chief's eye flashed ; his plans
   Soared up again like fire.

The chief's eye flashed ; but presently
   Softened itself, as sheathes
A film the mother-eagle's eye
   When her bruised eaglet breathes :
" You're wounded ! "   " Nay," the soldier's pride
   Touched to the quick, he said :
" I'm killed, Sire ! "   And his chief beside,
   Smiling the boy fell dead.

                 ROBERT BROWNING.

THE PATRIOT

AN OLD STORY

IT was roses, roses, all the way,
   With myrtle mixed in my path like mad :
The house-roofs seemed to heave and sway,
   The church-spires flamed, such flags they had,
A year ago on this very day.

The air broke into a mist with bells,
   The old walls rocked with the crowd and cries.

Had I said, " Good folk, mere noise repels—
    But give me your sun from yonder skies ! "
They had answered, " And afterward, what else ? "

Alack, it was I who leaped at the sun
    To give it my loving friends to keep !
Nought man could do, have I left undone :
    And you see my harvest, what I reap
This very day, now a year is run.

There's nobody on the house-tops now—
    Just a palsied few at the windows set ;
For the best of the sight is, all allow,
    At the Shambles' Gate—or, better yet,
By the very scaffold's foot, I trow.

I go in the rain, and, more than needs,
    A rope cuts both my wrists behind ;
And I think, by the feel, my forehead bleeds,
    For they fling, whoever has a mind,
Stones at me for my year's misdeeds.

Thus I entered, and thus I go !
    In triumphs, people have dropped down dead.
" Paid by the world, what dost thou owe
    Me ? "—God might question ; now instead,
'Tis God shall repay : I am safer so.

ROBERT BROWNING.

A GRAMMARIAN'S FUNERAL

SHORTLY AFTER THE REVIVAL OF LEARNING IN EUROPE

LET us begin and carry up this corpse,
    Singing together.
Leave we the common crofts, the vulgar thorpes,
    Each in its tether

Sleeping safe on the bosom of the plain,
    Cared-for till cock-crow :
Look out if yonder be not day again
    Rimming the rock-row !
That's the appropriate country ; there, man's thought,
    Rarer, intenser,
Self-gathered for an outbreak, as it ought,
    Chafes in the censer.
Leave we the unlettered plain its herd and crop ;
    Seek we sepulture
On a tall mountain, citied to the top,
    Crowded with culture !
All the peaks soar, but one the rest excels ;
    Clouds overcome it ;
No, yonder sparkle is the citadel's
    Circling its summit.
Thither our path lies ; wind we up the heights :
    Wait ye the warning ?
Our low life was the level's and the night's ;
    He's for the morning.
Step to a tune, square chests, erect each head,
    'Ware the beholders !
This is our master, famous, calm and dead,
    Borne on our shoulders.

Sleep, crop and herd ! sleep, darkling thorpe and croft
    Safe from the weather !
He, whom we convoy to his grave aloft,
    Singing together,
He was a man born with thy face and throat,
    Lyric Apollo !
Long he lived nameless : how should spring take note
    Winter would follow ?
Till lo, the little touch, and youth was gone !
    Cramped and diminished,
Moaned he, " New measures, other feet anon !
    My dance is finished ? "

No, that's the world's way : (keep the mountain-side,
      Make for the city !)
He knew the signal, and stepped on with pride
      Over men's pity ;
Left play for work, and grappled with the world
      Bent on escaping :
"What's in the scroll," quoth he, " thou keepest furled?
      Show me their shaping,
Theirs who most studied man, the bard and sage,—
      Give ! "—So, he gowned him,
Straight got by heart that book to its last page :
      Learned, we found him.
Yea, but we found him bald too, eyes like lead,
      Accents uncertain :
" Time to taste life," another would have said,
      " Up with the curtain ! "
This man said rather, " Actual life comes next ?
      Patience a moment !
Grant I have mastered learning's crabbed text,
      Still there's the comment.
Let me know all !   Prate not of most or least,
      Painful or easy !
Even to the crumbs I'd fain eat up the feast,
      Ay, nor feel queasy."
Oh, such a life as he resolved to live,
      When he had learned it,
When he had gathered all books had to give !
      Sooner, he spurned it.
Image the whole, then execute the parts—
      Fancy the fabric
Quite, ere you build, ere steel strike fire from quartz,
      Ere mortar dab brick !

(Here's the town-gate reached : there's the market-
      place
      Gaping before us.)
Yea, this in him was the peculiar grace
      (Hearten our chorus !)

That before living he'd learn how to live—
    No end to learning :
Earn the means first—God surely will contrive
    Use for our earning.
Others mistrust and say, " But time escapes :
    Live now or never ! "
He said, " What's time ? Leave Now for dogs and apes !
    Man has Forever."
Back to his book then : deeper drooped his head :
    Calculus racked him :
Leaden before, his eyes grew dross of lead :
    Tussis attacked him.
" Now, master, take a little rest ! "—not he !
    (Caution redoubled,
Step two a-breast, the way winds narrowly !)
    Not a whit troubled,
Back to his studies, fresher than at first,
    Fierce as a dragon
He (soul-hydroptic with a sacred thirst)
    Sucked at the flagon.
Oh, if we draw a circle premature,
    Heedless of far gain,
Greedy for quick returns of profit, sure
    Bad is our bargain !
Was it not great ? did not he throw on God,
    (He loves the burthen)—
God's task to make the heavenly period
    Perfect the earthen ?
Did not he magnify the mind, show clear
    Just what it all meant ?
He would not discount life, as fools do here,
    Paid by instalment.
He ventured neck or nothing—heaven's success
    Found, or earth's failure :
" Wilt thou trust death or not ? " He answered " Yes !
    Hence with life's pale lure ! "
That low man seeks a little thing to do,
    Sees it and does it :

This high man, with a great thing to pursue,
    Dies ere he knows it.
That low man goes on adding one to one,
    His hundred's soon hit :
This high man, aiming at a million,
    Misses an unit.
That, has the world here—should he need the next,
    Let the world mind him !
This, throws himself on God, and unperplexed
    Seeking shall find him.
So, with the throttling hands of death at strife,
    Ground he at grammar ;
Still, thro' the rattle, parts of speech were rife :
    While he could stammer
He settled *Hoti's* business—let it be !—
    Properly based *Oun*—
Gave us the doctrine of the enclitic *De*,
    Dead from the waist down.
Well, here's the platform, here's the proper place :
    Hail to your purlieus,
All ye highfliers of the feathered race,
    Swallows and curlews !
Here's the top-peak ; the multitude below
    Live, for they can, there :
This man decided not to Live but Know—
    Bury this man there ?
Here—here's his place, where meteors shoot, clouds
       form,
    Lightnings are loosened,
Stars come and go !   Let joy break with the storm,
    Peace let the dew send !
Lofty designs must close in like effects :
    Loftily lying,
Leave him—still loftier than the world suspects,
    Living and dying.

                        ROBERT BROWNING.

THE LADY OF SHALOTT

PART I

On either side the river lie
Long fields of barley and of rye,
That clothe the wold and meet the sky;
And through the field the road runs by
          To many-tower'd Camelot;
And up and down the people go,
Gazing where the lilies blow
Round an island there below,
          The island of Shalott.

Willows whiten, aspens quiver,
Little breezes dusk and shiver
Through the wave that runs for ever
By the island in the river
          Flowing down to Camelot.
Four grey walls, and four grey towers,
Overlook a space of flowers,
And the silent isle embowers
          The Lady of Shalott.

By the margin, willow-veil'd
Slide the heavy barges trail'd
By slow horses; and unhail'd
The shallop flitteth silken-sail'd
          Skimming down to Camelot:
But who hath seen her wave her hand?
Or at the casement seen her stand?
Or is she known in all the land,
          The Lady of Shalott?

Only reapers, reaping early
In among the bearded barley,

Hear a song that echoes cheerly
From the river winding clearly,
  Down to tower'd Camelot:
And by the moon the reaper weary,
Piling sheaves in uplands airy,
Listening, whispers " 'Tis the fairy
  Lady of Shalott."

PART II

There she weaves by night and day
A magic web with colours gay.
She has heard a whisper say,
A curse is on her if she stay
  To look down to Camelot.
She knows not what the curse may be,
And so she weaveth steadily,
And little other care hath she,
  The Lady of Shalott.

And moving through a mirror clear
That hangs before her all the year,
Shadows of the world appear.
There she sees the highway near
  Winding down to Camelot:
There the river eddy whirls,
And there the surly village-churls,
And the red cloaks of market girls,
  Pass onward from Shalott.

Sometimes a troop of damsels glad,
An abbot on an ambling pad,
Sometimes a curly shepherd-lad,
Or long-hair'd page in crimson clad,
  Goes by to tower'd Camelot;
And sometimes through the mirror blue
The knights come riding two and two:
She hath no loyal knight and true,
  The Lady of Shalott.

But in her web she still delights
To weave the mirror's magic sights,
For often through the silent nights
A funeral, with plumes and lights,
      And music, went to Camelot:
Or when the moon was overhead,
Came two young lovers lately wed;—
"I am half sick of shadows," said
      The Lady of Shalott.

PART III

A bow-shot from her bower-eaves,
He rode between the barley-sheaves;
The sun came dazzling through the leaves,
And flamed upon the brazen greaves
      Of bold Sir Lancelot.
A red-cross knight for ever kneel'd
To a lady in his shield,
That sparkled on the yellow field
      Beside remote Shalott.

The gemmy bridle glitter'd free,
Like to some branch of stars we see
Hung in the golden Galaxy.
The bridle bells rang merrily
      As he rode down to Camelot:
And from his blazon'd baldric slung
A mighty silver bugle hung,
And as he rode his armour rung
      Beside remote Shalott.

All in the blue unclouded weather
Thick-jewell'd shone the saddle-leather,
The helmet and the helmet-feather
Burn'd like one burning flame together,
      As he rode down to Camelot:

As often through the purple night,
Below the starry clusters bright,
Some bearded meteor, trailing light,
     Moves over still Shalott.

His broad clear brow in sunlight glow'd ;
On burnish'd hooves his war-horse trode ;
From underneath his helmet flow'd
His coal-black curls as on he rode,
     As he rode down to Camelot.
From the bank and from the river
He flash'd into the crystal mirror,
" Tirra lirra," by the river
     Sang Sir Lancelot.

She left the web, she left the loom,
She made three paces through the room,
She saw the water-lily bloom,
She saw the helmet and the plume,
     She look'd down to Camelot.
Out flew the web and floated wide ;
The mirror crack'd from side to side :
" The curse is come upon me," cried
     The Lady of Shalott.

PART IV

In the stormy east-wind straining,
The pale yellow woods were waning,
The broad stream in his banks complaining,
Heavily the low sky raining
     Over tower'd Camelot ;
Down she came and found a boat
Beneath a willow left afloat,
And round about the prow she wrote
     The Lady of Shalott.

And down the river's dim expanse—
Like some bold seër in a trance,

Seeing all his own mischance—
With a glassy countenance
  Did she look to Camelot.
And at the closing of the day
She loosed the chain, and down she lay;
The broad stream bore her far away,
  The Lady of Shalott.

Lying, robed in snowy white
That loosely flew to left and right—
The leaves upon her falling light—
Through the noises of the night
  She floated down to Camelot:
And as the boat-head wound along
The willowy hills and fields among,
They heard her singing her last song,
  The Lady of Shalott—

Heard a carol, mournful, holy,
Chanted loudly, chanted lowly,
Till her blood was frozen slowly,
And her eyes were darken'd wholly,
  Turn'd to tower'd Camelot;
For ere she reach'd upon the tide
The first house by the water-side,
Singing in her song she died,
  The Lady of Shalott.

Under tower and balcony,
By garden-wall and gallery,
A gleaming shape she floated by,
Dead-pale between the houses high,
  Silent into Camelot.
Out upon the wharfs they came,
Knight and burgher, lord and dame,
And round the prow they read her name,
  The Lady of Shalott.

Who is this, and what is here ?
And in the lighted palace near
Died the sound of royal cheer ;
And they cross'd themselves for fear,
   All the knights at Camelot :
But Lancelot mused a little space ;
He said, " She has a lovely face ;
God in his mercy lend her grace,
   The Lady of Shalott."

        LORD TENNYSON.

ŒNONE

THERE lies a vale in Ida, lovelier
Than all the valleys of Ionian hills.
The swimming vapour slopes athwart the glen,
Puts forth an arm, and creeps from pine to pine
And loiters, slowly drawn. On either hand
The lawns and meadow-ledges midway down
Hang rich in flowers, and far below them roars
The long brook falling through the clov'n ravine
In cataract after cataract to the sea.
Behind the valley topmost Gargarus
Stands up and takes the morning : but in front
The gorges, opening wide apart, reveal
Troas and Ilion's column'd citadel,
The crown of Troas.
       Hither came at noon
Mournful Œnone, wandering forlorn
Of Paris, once her playmate on the hills.
Her cheek had lost the rose, and round her neck
Floated her hair or seem'd to float in rest.
She, leaning on a fragment twined with vine,
Sang to the stillness, till the mountain-shade
Sloped downward to her seat from the upper cliff.

" O mother Ida, many-fountain'd Ida,
Dear mother Ida, harken ere I die.

For now the noonday quiet holds the hill :
The grasshopper is silent in the grass :
The lizard, with his shadow on the stone,
Rests like a shadow, and the cicala sleeps.
The purple flowers droop : the golden bee
Is lily-cradled : I alone awake.
My eyes are full of tears, my heart of love,
My heart is breaking, and my eyes are dim,
And I am all aweary of my life.

" O mother Ida, many fountain'd Ida,
Dear mother Ida, harken ere I die.
Hear me, O Earth, hear me, O Hills, O Caves,
That house the gold-crown'd snake ! O mountain
    brooks,
I am the daughter of a River-God,
Hear me, for I will speak, and build up all
My sorrow with my song, as yonder walls
Rose slowly to a music slowly breathed,
A cloud that gather'd shape : for it may be
That, while I speak of it, a little while
My heart may wander from its deeper woe.

" O mother Ida, many-fountain'd Ida,
Dear mother Ida, harken ere I die.
I waited underneath the dawning hills,
Aloft the mountain lawn was dewy-dark,
And dewy-dark aloft the mountain pine :
Beautiful Paris, evil-hearted Paris,
Leading a jet-black goat white-horn'd, white-hooved,
Came up from reedy Simois all alone.

" O mother Ida, harken ere I die.
Far-off the torrent call'd me from the cleft :
Far up the solitary morning smote
The streaks of virgin snow.   With down-dropt eyes
I sat alone : white-breasted like a star
Fronting the dawn he moved ; a leopard skin

Droop'd from his shoulder, but his sunny hair
Cluster'd about his temples like a God's ;
And his cheek brighten'd as the foam-bow brightens
When the wind blows the foam, and all my heart
Went forth to embrace him coming ere he came.

" Dear mother Ida, harken ere I die.
He smiled, and opening out his milk-white palm
Disclosed a fruit of pure Hesperian gold,
That smelt ambrosially, and while I look'd
And listen'd, the full-flowing river of speech
Came down upon my heart.

                              " ' My own Œnone,
Beautiful-brow'd Œnone, my own soul,
Behold this fruit, whose gleaming rind ingrav'n
" For the most fair," would seem to award it thine,
As lovelier than whatever Oread haunt
The knolls of Ida, loveliest in all grace
Of movement, and the charm of married brows.'

" Dear mother Ida, harken ere I die.
He prest the blossom of his lips to mine,
And added, ' This was cast upon the board,
When all the full-faced presence of the Gods
Ranged in the halls of Peleus ; whereupon
Rose feud, with question unto whom 'twere due :
But light-foot Iris brought it yester-eve,
Delivering, that to me, by common voice
Elected umpire, Herè comes to-day,
Pallas and Aphrodite, claiming each
This meed of fairest. Thou, within the cave
Behind yon whispering tuft of oldest pine,
Mayst well behold them unbeheld, unheard
Hear all, and see thy Paris judge of Gods.'

" Dear mother Ida, harken ere I die.
It was the deep midnoon : one silvery cloud
Had lost his way between the piney sides

Of this long glen.   Then to the bower they came,
Naked they came to that smooth-swarded bower,
And at their feet the crocus brake like fire,
Violet, amaracus, and asphodel,
Lotus and lilies : and a wind arose,
And overhead the wandering ivy and vine,
This way and that, in many a wild festoon
Ran riot, garlanding the gnarled boughs
With bunch and berry and flower through and through.

" O mother Ida, harken ere I die.
On the tree-tops a crested peacock lit,
And o'er him flow'd a golden cloud, and lean'd
Upon him, slowly dropping fragrant dew.
Then first I heard the voice of her, to whom
Coming through Heaven, like a light that grows
Larger and clearer, with one mind the Gods
Rise up for reverence.   She to Paris made
Proffer of royal power, ample rule
Unquestion'd, overflowing revenue
Wherewith to embellish state, ' From many a vale
And river-sunder'd champaign clothed with corn,
Or labour'd mines undrainable of ore.
Honour,' she said, ' and homage, tax and toll,
From many an inland town and haven large,
Mast-throng'd beneath her shadowing citadel
In glassy bays among her tallest towers.'

" O mother Ida, harken ere I die.
Still she spake on, and still she spake of power,
' Which in all action is the end of all ;
Power fitted to the season ; wisdom-bred
And throned of wisdom—from all neighbour crowns
Alliance and allegiance, till thy hand
Fail from the sceptre-staff.   Such boon from me,
From me, Heaven's Queen, Paris, to thee king-born,
A shepherd all thy life, but yet king-born,
Should come most welcome, seeing men, in power

(2,599)

4

Only, are likest gods, who have attain'd
Rest in a happy place and quiet seats
Above the thunder, with undying bliss
In knowledge of their own supremacy.'

" Dear mother Ida, harken ere I die.
She ceased, and Paris held the costly fruit
Out at arm's-length, so much the thought of power
Flatter'd his spirit ; but Pallas where she stood,
Somewhat apart, her clear and bared limbs
O'erthwarted with the brazen-headed spear
Upon her pearly shoulder leaning cold,
The while, above, her full and earnest eye
Over her snow-cold breast and angry cheek
Kept watch, waiting decision, made reply.

" ' Self-reverence, self-knowledge, self-control,
These three alone lead life to sovereign power.
Yet not for power (power of herself
Would come uncall'd for), but to live by law,
Acting the law we live by without fear ;
And, because right is right, to follow right
Were wisdom in the scorn of consequence.'

" Dear mother Ida, harken ere I die.
Again she said : ' I woo thee not with gifts.
Sequel of guerdon could not alter me
To fairer.   Judge thou me by what I am,
So shalt thou find me fairest.

                       Yet, indeed,
If gazing on divinity disrobed
Thy mortal eyes are frail to judge of fair,
Unbiass'd by self-profit, oh ! rest thee sure
That I shall love thee well and cleave to thee,
So that my vigour, wedded to thy blood,
Shall strike within thy pulses, like a God's,
To push thee forward through a life of shocks,
Dangers, and deeds, until endurance grow

Sinew'd with action, and the full-grown will,
Circled through all experiences, pure law,
Commeasure perfect freedom.'

                " Here she ceased,
And Paris ponder'd, and I cried, ' O Paris,
Give it to Pallas ! ' but he heard me not,
Or hearing would not hear me, woe is me !

" O mother Ida, many-fountain'd Ida,
Dear mother Ida, harken ere I die.
Idalian Aphrodite beautiful,
Fresh as the foam, new-bathed in Paphian wells,
With rosy slender fingers backward drew
From her warm brows and bosom her deep hair
Ambrosial, golden round her lucid throat
And shoulder : from the violets her light foot
Shone rosy-white, and o'er her rounded form
Between the shadows of the vine-bunches
Floated the glowing sunlights, as she moved.

" Dear mother Ida, harken ere I die.
She with a subtle smile in her mild eyes,
The herald of her triumph, drawing nigh
Half-whispered in his ear, ' I promise thee
The fairest and most loving wife in Greece.'
She spoke and laugh'd : I shut my sight for fear :
But when I look'd, Paris had raised his arm,
And I beheld great Herè's angry eyes,
As she withdrew into the golden cloud,
And I was left alone within the bower ;
And from that time to this I am alone,
And I shall be alone until I die.

" Yet, mother Ida, harken ere I die.
Fairest—why fairest wife ? am I not fair ?
My love hath told me so a thousand times.
Methinks I must be fair, for yesterday,
When I pass'd by, a wild and wanton pard,

Eyed like the evening star, with playful tail
Crouch'd fawning in the weed.   Most loving is she ?
Ah me, my mountain shepherd, that my arms
Were wound about thee, and my hot lips prest
Close, close to thine in that quick-falling dew
Of fruitful kisses, thick as Autumn rains
Flash in the pools of whirling Simois.

" O mother, hear me yet before I die.
They came, they cut away my tallest pines,
My dark tall pines, that plumed the craggy ledge
High over the blue gorge, and all between
The snowy peak and snow-white cataract
Foster'd the callow eaglet—from beneath
Whose thick mysterious boughs in the dark morn,
The panther's roar came muffled, while I sat
Low in the valley.   Never, never more
Shall lone Œnone see the morning mist
Sweep through them ; never see them overlaid
With narrow moonlit slips of silver cloud,
Between the loud stream and the trembling stars.

" O mother, hear me yet before I die.
I wish that somewhere in the ruin'd folds,
Among the fragments tumbled from the glens
Or the dry thickets, I could meet with her,
The Abominable, that uninvited came
Into the fair Peleïan banquet-hall,
And cast the golden fruit upon the board,
And bred this change ; that I might speak my mind,
And tell her to her face how much I hate
Her presence, hated both of Gods and men.

" O mother, hear me yet before I die.
Hath he not sworn his love a thousand times,
In this green valley, under this green hill,
Ev'n on this hand, and sitting on this stone ?
Seal'd it with kisses ? water'd it with tears ?

O happy tears, and how unlike to these !
O happy Heaven, how canst thou see my face ?
O happy earth, how canst thou bear my weight ?
O death, death, death, thou ever-floating cloud,
There are enough unhappy on this earth,
Pass by the happy souls, that love to live :
I pray thee, pass before my light of life,
And shadow all my soul, that I may die.
Thou weighest heavy on the heart within,
Weigh heavy on my eyelids : let me die.

" O mother, hear me yet before I die.
I will not die alone, for fiery thoughts
Do shape themselves within me, more and more,
Whereof I catch the issue, as I hear
Dead sounds at night come from the inmost hills,
Like footsteps upon wool.   I dimly see
My far-off doubtful purpose, as a mother
Conjectures of the features of her child
Ere it is born : her child !—a shudder comes
Across me : never child be born of me,
Unblest, to vex me with his father's eyes !

" O mother, hear me yet before I die.
Hear me, O earth.   I will not die alone,
Lest their shrill happy laughter come to me
Walking the cold and starless road of Death
Uncomforted, leaving my ancient love
With the Greek woman.   I will rise and go
Down into Troy, and ere the stars come forth
Talk with the wild Cassandra, for she says
A fire dances before her, and a sound
Rings ever in her ears of armed men.
What this may be I know not, but I know
That, wheresoe'er I am by night and day,
All earth and air seem only burning fire."
                                        LORD TENNYSON.

THE LOTOS-EATERS

" Courage ! " he said, and pointed toward the land,
" This mounting wave will roll us shoreward soon."
In the afternoon they came unto a land,
In which it seemed always afternoon.
All round the coast the languid air did swoon,
Breathing like one that hath a weary dream.
Full-faced above the valley stood the moon ;
And like a downward smoke, the slender stream
Along the cliff to fall and pause and fall did seem.

A land of streams ! some, like a downward smoke,
Slow-dropping veils of thinnest lawn, did go ;
And some through wavering lights and shadows broke,
Rolling a slumbrous sheet of foam below.
They saw the gleaming river seaward flow
From the inner land : far off, three mountain-tops,
Three silent pinnacles of aged snow,
Stood sunset-flush'd : and, dew'd with showery drops,
Up-clomb the shadowy pine above the woven copse.

The charmed sunset linger'd low adown
In the red West : through mountain clefts the dale
Was seen far inland, and the yellow down
Border'd with palm, and many a winding vale
And meadow, set with slender galingale ;
A land where all things always seem'd the same !
And round about the keel with faces pale,
Dark faces pale against that rosy flame,
The mild-eyed melancholy Lotos-eaters came.

Branches they bore of that enchanted stem,
Laden with flower and fruit, whereof they gave
To each, but whoso did receive of them,
And taste, to him the gushing of the wave
Far far away did seem to mourn and rave
On alien shores ; and if his fellow spake,

His voice was thin, as voices from the grave ;
And deep asleep he seem'd, yet all awake,
And music in his ears his beating heart did make.

They sat them down upon the yellow sand,
Between the sun and moon upon the shore ;
And sweet it was to dream of Fatherland,
Of child, and wife, and slave ; but evermore
Most weary seem'd the sea, weary the oar,
Weary the wandering fields of barren foam.
Then some one said, " We will return no more ; "
And all at once they sang, " Our island home
Is far beyond the wave ; we will no longer roam."

CHORIC SONG

I

There is sweet music here that softer falls
Than petals from blown roses on the grass,
Or night-dews on still waters between walls
Of shadowy granite, in a gleaming pass ;
Music that gentlier on the spirit lies,
Than tir'd eyelids upon tir'd eyes ;
Music that brings sweet sleep down from the blissful
    skies.
Here are cool mosses deep,
And through the moss the ivies creep,
And in the stream the long-leaved flowers weep,
And from the craggy ledge the poppy hangs in sleep.

II

Why are we weigh'd upon with heaviness,
And utterly consumed with sharp distress,
While all things else have rest from weariness ?
All things have rest : why should we toil alone,
We only toil, who are the first of things,
And make perpetual moan,
Still from one sorrow to another thrown :

Nor ever fold our wings,
And cease from wanderings,
Nor steep our brows in slumber's holy balm ;
Nor harken what the inner spirit sings,
" There is no joy but calm ! "
Why should we only toil, the roof and crown of things?

III

Lo ! in the middle of the wood,
The folded leaf is woo'd from out the bud
With winds upon the branch, and there
Grows green and broad, and takes no care,
Sun-steep'd at noon, and in the moon
Nightly dew-fed ; and turning yellow
Falls, and floats adown the air.
Lo ! sweeten'd with the summer light,
The full-juiced apple, waxing over-mellow,
Drops in a silent autumn night,
All its allotted length of days,
The flower ripens in its place,
Ripens and fades, and falls, and hath no toil,
Fast-rooted in the fruitful soil.

IV

Hateful is the dark-blue sky,
Vaulted o'er the dark-blue sea.
Death is the end of life ; ah, why
Should life all labour be ?
Let us alone. Time driveth onward fast,
And in a little while our lips are dumb.
Let us alone. What is it that will last ?
All things are taken from us, and become
Portions and parcels of the dreadful Past.
Let us alone. What pleasure can we have
To war with evil ? Is there any peace
In ever climbing up the climbing wave ?
All things have rest, and ripen toward the grave

In silence ; ripen, fall and cease :
Give us long rest or death, dark death, or dreamful ease.

V

How sweet it were, hearing the downward stream,
  With half-shut eyes ever to seem
  Falling asleep in a half-dream !
To dream and dream, like yonder amber light,
Which will not leave the myrrh-bush on the height ;
To hear each other's whisper'd speech ;
  Eating the Lotos day by day,
To watch the crisping ripples on the beach,
And tender curving lines of creamy spray ;
  To lend our hearts and spirits wholly
To the influence of mild-minded melancholy ;
To muse and brood and live again in memory,
  With those old faces of our infancy
  Heap'd over with a mound of grass,
Two handfuls of white dust, shut in an urn of brass !

VI

Dear is the memory of our wedded lives,
And dear the last embraces of our wives
And their warm tears : but all hath suffer'd change ;
For surely now our household hearths are cold :
Our sons inherit us : our looks are strange :
And we should come like ghosts to trouble joy.
Or else the island princes over-bold
Have eat our substance, and the minstrel sings
Before them of the ten years' war in Troy,
And our great deeds, as half-forgotten things.
Is there confusion in the little isle ?
Let what is broken so remain.
The Gods are hard to reconcile :
'Tis hard to settle order once again.
There *is* confusion worse than death,
Trouble on trouble, pain on pain,

Long labour unto aged breath,
Sore task to hearts worn out with many wars
And eyes grown dim with gazing on the pilot-stars.

VII

But propt on beds of amaranth and moly,
How sweet (while warm airs lull us, blowing lowly)
With half-dropt eyelids still,
Beneath a heaven dark and holy,
To watch the long bright river drawing slowly
His waters from the purple hill—
To hear the dewy echoes calling
From cave to cave through the thick-twined vine—
To watch the emerald-colour'd water falling
Through many a woven acanthus-wreath divine !
Only to hear and see the far-off sparkling brine,
Only to hear were sweet, stretch'd out beneath the pine.

VIII

The Lotos blooms below the barren peak :
The Lotos blows by every winding creek :
All day the wind breathes low with mellower tone :
Through every hollow cave and alley lone
Round and round the spicy downs the yellow Lotos-
    dust is blown.
We have had enough of action, and of motion we,
Roll'd to starboard, roll'd to larboard, when the surge
    was seething free,
Where the wallowing monster spouted his foam-
    fountains in the sea.
Let us swear an oath, and keep it with an equal mind,
In the hollow Lotos-land to live and lie reclined
On the hills like Gods together, careless of mankind.
For they lie beside their nectar, and the bolts are hurl'd
Far below them in the valleys, and the clouds are
    lightly curl'd
Round their golden houses, girdled with the gleaming
    world :

Where they smile in secret, looking over wasted lands,
Blight and famine, plague and earthquake, roaring
    deeps and fiery sands,
Clanging fights, and flaming towns, and sinking ships,
    and praying hands.
But they smile, they find a music centred in a doleful
    song
Steaming up, a lamentation and an ancient tale of
    wrong,
Like a tale of little meaning though the words are
    strong ;
Chanted from an ill-used race of men that cleave the
    soil,
Sow the seed, and reap the harvest with enduring toil,
Storing yearly little dues of wheat, and wine and oil ;
Till they perish and they suffer—some, 'tis whisper'd,
    down in hell
Suffer endless anguish, others in Elysian valleys dwell,
Resting weary limbs at last on beds of asphodel.
Surely, surely, slumber is more sweet than toil, the
    shore
Than labour in the deep mid-ocean, wind and wave
    and oar :
O rest ye, brother mariners, we will not wander more !

LORD TENNYSON.

LYRICS FROM "THE PRINCESS"

I

Sweet and low, sweet and low,
    Wind of the western sea,
Low, low, breathe and blow,
    Wind of the western sea !
Over the rolling waters go,
Come from the dying moon, and blow,
    Blow him again to me ;
While my little one, while my pretty one, sleeps.

Sleep and rest, sleep and rest,
    Father will come to thee soon ;
Rest, rest, on mother's breast,
    Father will come to thee soon ;
Father will come to his babe in the nest,
Silver sails all out of the west
    Under the silver moon :
Sleep, my little one, sleep, my pretty one, sleep.

II

The splendour falls on castle walls
    And snowy summits old in story ;
The long light shakes across the lakes,
    And the wild cataract leaps in glory.
Blow, bugle, blow, set the wild echoes flying,
Blow, bugle ; answer, echoes, dying, dying, dying.

O hark, O hear ! how thin and clear,
    And thinner, clearer, farther going !
O sweet and far from cliff and scar
    The horns of Elfland faintly blowing !
Blow, let us hear the purple glens replying :
Blow, bugle ; answer, echoes, dying, dying, dying.

O love, they die in yon rich sky ;
    They faint on hill or field or river :
Our echoes roll from soul to soul,
    And grow for ever and for ever.
Blow, bugle, blow, set the wild echoes flying,
And answer, echoes, answer, dying, dying, dying.

III

" Tears, idle tears, I know not what they mean,
Tears from the depth of some divine despair
Rise in the heart, and gather to the eyes,
In looking on the happy Autumn fields,
And thinking of the days that are no more.

" Fresh as the first beam glittering on a sail,
That brings our friends up from the underworld,
Sad as the last which reddens over one
That sinks with all we love below the verge ;
So sad, so fresh, the days that are no more.

" Ah, sad and strange as in dark summer dawns
The earliest pipe of half-awaken'd birds
To dying ears, when unto dying eyes
The casement slowly grows a glimmering square ;
So sad, so strange, the days that are no more.

" Dear as remember'd kisses after death,
And sweet as those by hopeless fancy feign'd
On lips that are for others ; deep as love,
Deep as first love, and wild with all regret ;
O Death in Life, the days that are no more."

IV

" Now sleeps the crimson petal, now the white :
Nor waves the cypress in the palace walk ;
Nor winks the gold fin in the porphyry font :
The fire-fly wakens : waken thou with me.

" Now droops the milkwhite peacock like a ghost,
And like a ghost she glimmers on to me.

" Now lies the Earth all Danaë to the stars,
And all thy heart lies open unto me.

" Now slides the silent meteor on, and leaves
A shining furrow, as thy thoughts in me.

" Now folds the lily all her sweetness up,
And slips into the bosom of the lake ;
So fold thyself, my dearest, thou, and slip
Into my bosom and be lost in me."

LORD TENNYSON.

PART II

PATRIOTIC POEMS

HOME-THOUGHTS, FROM ABROAD

OH, to be in England
Now that April's there,
And whoever wakes in England
Sees, some morning, unaware,
That the lowest boughs and the brush-wood sheaf
Round the elm-tree bole are in tiny leaf,
While the chaffinch sings on the orchard bough
In England—now !

And after April, when May follows,
And the whitethroat builds, and all the swallows !
Hark, where my blossomed pear-tree in the hedge
Leans to the field and scatters on the clover
Blossoms and dewdrops—at the bent spray's edge—
That's the wise thrush ; he sings each song twice over,
Lest you should think he never could recapture
The first fine careless rapture !

And though the fields look rough with hoary dew,
All will be gay when noontide wakes anew
The buttercups, the little children's dower
—Far brighter than this gaudy melon-flower !

ROBERT BROWNING.

TO J. S.

(EXTRACTS.)

You ask me why, though ill at ease,
 Within this region I subsist,
 Whose spirits falter in the mist,
And languish for the purple seas?

It is the land that freemen till,
 That sober-suited Freedom chose,
 The land, where girt with friends or foes
A man may speak the thing he will;

A land of settled government,
 A land of just and old renown,
 Where Freedom slowly broadens down
From precedent to precedent:

Where faction seldom gathers head,
 But by degrees to fullness wrought,
 The strength of some diffusive thought
Hath time and space to work and spread.

Should banded unions persecute
 Opinion, and induce a time
 When single thought is civil crime,
And individual freedom mute;

Though Power should make from land to land
 The name of Britain trebly great—
 Though every channel of the State
Should almost choke with golden sand—

Yet waft me from the harbour-mouth,
 Wild wind! I seek a warmer sky,
 And I will see before I die
The palms and temples of the South.

Of old sat Freedom on the heights,
    The thunders breaking at her feet :
Above her shook the starry lights :
    She heard the torrents meet.

There in her place she did rejoice,
    Self-gather'd in her prophet-mind ;
But fragments of her mighty voice
    Came rolling on the wind.

Then stept she down through town and field
    To mingle with the human race,
And part by part to men reveal'd
    The fullness of her face—

Grave mother of majestic works,
    From her isle-altar gazing down,
Who, God-like, grasps the triple forks,
    And, King-like, wears the crown :

Her open eyes desire the truth,
    The wisdom of a thousand years
Is in them.   May perpetual youth
    Keep dry their light from tears ;

That her fair form may stand and shine,
    Make bright our days and light our dreams,
Turning to scorn with lips divine
    The falsehood of extremes !

Love thou thy land, with love far-brought
    From out the storied Past, and used
    Within the Present, but tranfused
Through future time by power of thought.

True love turn'd round on fixed poles,
  Love that endures not sordid ends,
  For English natures, freemen, friends,
Thy brothers and immortal souls.

But pamper not a hasty time,
  Nor feed with crude imaginings
  The herd, wild hearts and feeble wings
That every sophister can lime.

Deliver not the tasks of might
  To weakness, neither hide the ray
  From those, not blind, who wait for day,
Though sitting girt, with doubtful light.

Make knowledge circle with the winds ;
  But let her herald, Reverence, fly
  Before her to whatever sky
Bear seed of men and growth of minds.

Watch what main-currents draw the years :
  Cut Prejudice against the grain :
  But gentle words are always gain :
Regard the weakness of thy peers :

Nor toil for title, place, or touch
  Of pension, neither count on praise :
  It grows to guerdon after-days :
Nor deal in watchwords overmuch ;

Not clinging to some ancient saw ;
  Not master'd by some modern term ;
  Not swift nor slow to change, but firm :
And in its season bring the law ;

That from Discussion's lip may fall
  With Life, that, working strongly, binds—
  Set in all lights by many minds,
To close the interests of all.

(2,599)

For Nature also, cold and warm,
   And moist and dry, devising long,
   Through many agents making strong,
Matures the individual form.

Meet is it changes should control
   Our being, lest we rust in ease.
   We all are changed by still degrees,
All but the basis of the soul.

So let the change which comes be free
   To ingroove itself with that which flies,
   And work, a joint of state, that plies
Its office, moved with sympathy.

A saying, hard to shape in act ;
   For all the past of Time reveals
   A bridal dawn of thunder-peals,
Wherever Thought hath wedded Fact.

Ev'n now we hear with inward strife
   A motion toiling in the gloom—
   The Spirit of the years to come
Yearning to mix himself with Life.

A slow-develop'd strength awaits
   Completion in a painful school ;
   Phantoms of other forms of rule,
New Majesties of mighty States—

The warders of the growing hour,
   But vague in vapour, hard to mark ;
   And round them sea and air are dark
With great contrivances of Power.

Of many changes, aptly join'd,
   Is bodied forth the second whole.
   Regard gradation, lest the soul
Of Discord race the rising wind ;

A wind to puff your idol-fires,
　　And heap their ashes on the head ;
　　To shame the boast so often made,
That we are wiser than our sires.

Oh yet, if Nature's evil star
　　Drive men in manhood, as in youth,
　　To follow flying steps of Truth
Across the brazen bridge of war—

If New and Old, disastrous feud,
　　Must ever shock, like armed foes,
　　And this be true, till Time shall close,
That Principles are rain'd in blood ;

Not yet the wise of heart would cease
　　To hold his hope through shame and guilt,
　　But with his hand against the hilt,
Would pace the troubled land, like Peace ;

Not less, though dogs of Faction bay,
　　Would serve his kind in deed and word,
　　Certain, if knowledge bring the sword,
That knowledge takes the sword away—

Would love the gleams of good that broke
　　From either side, nor veil his eyes :
　　And if some dreadful need should rise
Would strike, and firmly, and one stroke :

To-morrow yet would reap to-day,
　　As we bear blossom of the dead ;
　　Earn well the thrifty months, nor wed
Raw Haste, half-sister to Delay.

LORD TENNYSON.

HOME-THOUGHTS, FROM THE SEA

NOBLY, nobly Cape Saint Vincent to the North-West
    died away ;
Sunset ran, one glorious blood-red, reeking into Cadiz
    Bay ;
Bluish 'mid the burning water, full in face Trafalgar
    lay ;
In the dimmest North-East distance dawned Gib-
    raltar grand and grey ;
" Here and here did England help me : how can I help
    England ? "—say,
Whoso turns as I, this evening, turn to God to praise
    and pray,
While Jove's planet rises yonder, silent over Africa.
                      ROBERT BROWNING.

THE CHARGE OF THE LIGHT BRIGADE

I

Half a league, half a league,
  Half a league onward,
All in the valley of Death
  Rode the six hundred.
" Forward, the Light Brigade !
Charge for the guns ! " he said :
Into the valley of Death
  Rode the six hundred.

II

" Forward, the Light Brigade ! "
Was there a man dismay'd ?
Not though the soldier knew
  Some one had blunder'd :

Theirs not to make reply,
Theirs not to reason why,
Theirs but to do and die :
Into the valley of Death
    Rode the six hundred.

III

Cannon to right of them,
Cannon to left of them,
Cannon in front of them
    Volley'd and thunder'd ;
Storm'd at with shot and shell,
Boldly they rode and well,
Into the jaws of Death,
Into the mouth of Hell
    Rode the six hundred.

IV

Flash'd all their sabres bare,
Flash'd as they turn'd in air,
Sabring the gunners there,
Charging an army, while
    All the world wonder'd :
Plunged in the battery-smoke,
Right through the line they broke ;
Cossack and Russian
Reel'd from the sabre-stroke
    Shatter'd and sunder'd.
Then they rode back—but not,
    Not the six hundred.

V

Cannon to right of them,
Cannon to left of them,
Cannon behind them
    Volley'd and thunder'd ;

Storm'd at with shot and shell,
While horse and hero fell,
They that had fought so well
Came through the jaws of Death,
Back from the mouth of Hell,
All that was left of them,
    Left of six hundred.

VI

When can their glory fade?
Oh the wild charge they made!
    All the world wonder'd.
Honour the charge they made!
Honour the Light Brigade,
    Noble six hundred!

LORD TENNYSON.

STRAFFORD

(EXTRACT.)

[The Earl of Strafford, having served Charles I. with blind and passionate loyalty, is impeached for high treason by the Roundheads. The King, deserting Strafford, signs his death-warrant at the request of Pym.]

[As STRAFFORD *opens the door*, PYM *is discovered with* HAMPDEN, VANE, *etc.* STRAFFORD *falls back:* PYM *follows slowly and confronts him.*]

Pym. Have I done well? Speak, England! Whose
        sole sake
I still have laboured for, with disregard
To my own heart,—for whom my youth was made
Barren, my manhood waste, to offer up
Her sacrifice—this friend, this Wentworth here—
Who walked in youth with me, loved me, it may be
And whom, for his forsaking England's cause,
I hunted by all means (trusting that she

Would sanctify all means) even to the block
Which waits for him. And saying this, I feel
No bitterer pang than first I felt, the hour
I swore that Wentworth might leave us, but I
Would never leave him : I do leave him now.
I render up my charge (be witness, God !)
To England who imposed it. I have done
Her bidding—poorly, wrongly,—it may be,
With ill effects—for I am weak, a man :
Still, I have done my best, my human best,
Not faltering for a moment. It is done.
And this said, if I say . . . yes, I will say
I never loved but one man—David not
More Jonathan ! Even thus, I love him now :
And look for my chief portion in that world
Where great hearts led astray are turned again,
(Soon it may be, and, certes, will be soon :
My mission over, I shall not live long,)—
Ay, here I know I talk—I dare and must,
Of England, and her great reward, as all
I look for there ; but in my inmost heart,
Believe, I think of stealing quite away
To walk once more with Wentworth—my youth's
       friend
Purged from all error, gloriously renewed,
And Eliot shall not blame us. Then indeed . . .
This is no meeting, Wentworth ! Tears increase
Too hot. A thin mist—is it blood ?—enwraps
The face I loved once. Then, the meeting be !
    Straf. I have loved England too ; we'll meet then,
      Pym ;
As well die now ! Youth is the only time
To think and to decide on a great course :
Manhood with action follows ; but 'tis dreary,
To have to alter our whole life in age—
The time past, the strength gone ! As well die now.
When we meet, Pym, I'd be set right—not now !
Best die. Then if there's any fault, it too

Dies, smothered up. Poor grey old little Laud
May share his dream out, of a perfect Church,
In some blind corner. And there's no one left.
I trust the King now wholly to you, Pym !
And yet, I know not : I shall not be there :
Friends fail—if he have any. And he's weak,
And loves the Queen, and . . . Oh, my fate is nothing—
Nothing ! But not that awful head—not that !
   Pym. If England shall declare such will to me . . .
   Straf. Pym, you help England ! I, that am to die,
What I must see ! 'tis here—all here ! My God,
Let me but gasp out, in one word of fire,
How thou wilt plague him, satiating hell !
What ? England that you help, become through you
A green and putrefying charnel, left
Our children . . . some of us have children, Pym—
Some who, without that, still must ever wear
A darkened brow, an over-serious look,
And never properly be young ! No word ?
What if I curse you ? Send a strong curse forth
Clothed from my heart, lapped round with horror till
She's fit with her white face to walk the world
Scaring kind natures from your cause and you—
Then to sit down with you at the board-head,
The gathering for prayer . . . O speak, but speak !
. . . Creep up and quietly follow each one home,
You, you, you, be a nestling care for each
To sleep with,—hardly moaning in his dreams,
She gnaws so quietly,—till, lo he starts,
Gets off with half a heart eaten away !
Oh shall you 'scape with less if she's my child ?
You will not say a word—to me—to Him ?
   Pym. If England shall declare such will to me . . .
   Straf. No, not for England now, not for Heaven
     now,—
See, Pym, for my sake, mine who kneel to you !
There, I will thank you for the death, my friend !
This is the meeting : let me love you well !

Pym. England,—I am thine own ! Dost thou exact
That service ? I obey thee to the end.
Straf. O God, I shall die first—I shall die first !

ROBERT BROWNING.

ODE ON THE DEATH OF THE DUKE OF WELLINGTON

I

BURY the Great Duke
  With an empire's lamentation,
Let us bury the Great Duke
  To the noise of the mourning of a mighty nation,
Mourning when their leaders fall,
Warriors carry the warrior's pall,
And sorrow darkens hamlet and hall.

II

Where shall we lay the man whom we deplore ?
Here, in streaming London's central roar.
Let the sound of those he wrought for,
And the feet of those he fought for,
Echo round his bones for evermore.

III

Lead out the pageant : sad and slow,
As fits an universal woe,
Let the long long procession go,
And let the sorrowing crowd about it grow,
And let the mournful martial music blow ;
The last great Englishman is low.

IV

Mourn, for to us he seems the last,
Remembering all his greatness in the Past.

No more in soldier fashion will he greet
With lifted hand the gazer in the street.
O friends, our chief state-oracle is mute :
Mourn for the man of long-enduring blood,
The statesman-warrior, moderate, resolute,
Whole in himself, a common good,
Mourn for the man of amplest influence,
Yet clearest of ambitious crime,
Our greatest yet with least pretence,
Great in council and great in war,
Foremost captain of his time,
Rich in saving common-sense,
And, as the greatest only are,
In his simplicity sublime.
O good grey head which all men knew,
O voice from which their omens all men drew,
O iron nerve to true occasion true,
O fall'n at length that tower of strength
Which stood four-square to all the winds that blew !
Such was he whom we deplore.
The long self-sacrifice of life is o'er.
The great World-victor's victor will be seen no more.

v

All is over and done :
Render thanks to the Giver,
England, for thy son.
Let the bell be toll'd.
Render thanks to the Giver,
And render him to the mould.
Under the cross of gold
That shines over city and river,
There he shall rest for ever
Among the wise and the bold.
Let the bell be toll'd :
And a reverent people behold
The towering car, the sable steeds :
Bright let it be with his blazon'd deeds,

Dark in its funeral fold.
Let the bell be toll'd:
And a deeper knell in the heart be knoll'd;
And the sound of the sorrowing anthem roll'd
Through the dome of the golden cross;
And the volleying cannon thunder his loss;
He knew their voices of old.
For many a time in many a clime
His captain's ear has heard them boom
Bellowing victory, bellowing doom;
When he with those deep voices wrought,
Guarding realms and kings from shame;
With those deep voices our dead captain taught
The tyrant, and asserts his claim
In that dread sound to the great name,
Which he has worn so pure of blame,
In praise and in dispraise the same,
A man of well-attemper'd frame.
O civic muse, to such a name,
To such a name for ages long,
To such a name,
Preserve a broad approach of fame,
And ever-ringing avenues of song.

VI

Who is he that cometh, like an honour'd guest,
With banner and with music, with soldier and with
    priest,
With a nation weeping, and breaking on my rest?
Mighty seaman, this is he,
Was great by land as thou by sea.
Thine island loves thee well, thou famous man,
The greatest sailor since our world began.
Now, to the roll of muffled drums,
To thee the greatest soldier comes;
For this is he
Was great by land as thou by sea;

His foes were thine ; he kept us free ;
O give him welcome, this is he,
Worthy of our gorgeous rites,
And worthy to be laid by thee ;
For this is England's greatest son,
He that gain'd a hundred fights,
Nor ever lost an English gun ;
This is he that far away
Against the myriads of Assaye
Clash'd with his fiery few and won ;
And underneath another sun,
Warring on a later day,
Round affrighted Lisbon drew
The treble works, the vast designs
Of his labour'd rampart-lines,
Where he greatly stood at bay,
Whence he issued forth anew,
And ever great and greater grew,
Beating from the wasted vines
Back to France her banded swarms,
Back to France with countless blows,
Till o'er the hills her eagles flew
Past the Pyrenean pines,
Follow'd up in valley and glen
With blare of bugle, clamour of men,
Roll of cannon and clash of arms,
And England pouring on her foes.
Such a war had such a close.
Again their ravening eagle rose
In anger, wheel'd on Europe-shadowing wings,
And barking for the thrones of kings ;
Till one that sought but Duty's iron crown
On that loud Sabbath shook the spoiler down ;
A day of onsets of despair !
Dash'd on every rocky square
Their surging charges foam'd themselves away ;
Last, the Prussian trumpet blew ;
Through the long-tormented air

Heaven flash'd a sudden jubilant ray,
And down we swept and charged and overthrew.
So great a soldier taught us there,
What long-enduring hearts could do
In that world's-earthquake, Waterloo !
Mighty seaman, tender and true,
And pure as he from taint of craven guile,
O saviour of the silver-coasted isle,
O shaker of the Baltic and the Nile,
If aught of things that here befall
Touch a spirit among things divine,
If love of country move thee there at all,
Be glad, because his bones are laid by thine !
And through the centuries let a people's voice
In full acclaim,
A people's voice,
The proof and echo of all human fame,
A people's voice, when they rejoice
At civic revel and pomp and game,
Attest their great commander's claim
With honour, honour, honour, honour to him,
Eternal honour to his name.

VII

A people's voice ! we are a people yet.
Though all men else their nobler dreams forget,
Confused by brainless mobs and lawless Powers ;
Thank Him who isled us here, and roughly set
His Saxon in blown seas and storming showers,
We have a voice, with which to pay the debt
Of boundless love and reverence and regret
To those great men who fought, and kept it ours.
And keep it ours, O God, from brute control ;
O Statesmen, guard us, guard the eye, the soul
Of Europe, keep our noble England whole,
And save the one true seed of freedom sown
Betwixt a people and their ancient throne,

That sober freedom out of which there springs
Our loyal passion for our temperate kings ;
For, saving that, ye help to save mankind
Till public wrong be crumbled into dust,
And drill the raw world for the march of mind,
Till crowds at length be sane and crowns be just.
But wink no more in slothful overtrust.
Remember him who led your hosts ;
He bade you guard the sacred coasts.
Your cannons moulder on the seaward wall ;
His voice is silent in your council-hall
For ever ; and whatever tempests lour
For ever silent ; even if they broke
In thunder, silent ; yet remember all
He spoke among you, and the Man who spoke ;
Who never sold the truth to serve the hour,
Nor palter'd with Eternal God for power ;
Who let the turbid streams of rumour flow
Through either babbling world of high and low ;
Whose life was work, whose language rife
With rugged maxims hewn from life ;
Who never spoke against a foe :
Whose eighty winters freeze with one rebuke
All great self-seekers trampling on the right :
Truth-teller was our England's Alfred named ;
Truth-lover was our English Duke ;
Whatever record leap to light
He never shall be shamed.

VIII

Lo, the leader in these glorious wars
Now to glorious burial slowly borne,
Follow'd by the brave of other lands,
He, on whom from both her open hands
Lavish Honour shower'd all her stars,
And affluent Fortune emptied all her horn.
Yea, let all good things await

Him who cares not to be great,
But as he saves or serves the state.
Not once or twice in our rough island-story,
The path of duty was the way to glory :
He that walks it, only thirsting
For the right, and learns to deaden
Love of self, before his journey closes,
He shall find the stubborn thistle bursting
Into glossy purples, which outredden
All voluptuous garden-roses.
Not once or twice in our fair island-story,
The path of duty was the way to glory :
He, that ever following her commands,
On with toil of heart and knees and hands,
Through the long gorge to the far light has won
His path upward, and prevail'd,
Shall find the toppling crags of Duty scaled
Are close upon the shining table-lands
To which our God Himself is moon and sun.
Such was he : his work is done.
But while the races of mankind endure,
Let his great example stand
Colossal, seen of every land,
And keep the soldier firm, the statesman pure
Till in all lands and through all human story
The path of duty be the way to glory :
And let the land whose hearths he saved from shame
For many and many an age proclaim
At civic revel and pomp and game,
And when the long-illumined cities flame,
Their ever-loyal iron leader's fame,
With honour, honour, honour, honour to him,
Eternal honour to his name.

IX

Peace, his triumph will be sung
By some yet unmoulded tongue

Far on in summers that we shall not see :
Peace, it is a day of pain
For one about whose patriarchal knee
Late the little children clung :
O peace, it is a day of pain
For one, upon whose hand and heart and brain
Once the weight and fate of Europe hung.
Ours the pain, be his the gain !
More than is of man's degree
Must be with us, watching here
At this, our great solemnity.
Whom we see not we revere.
We revere, and we refrain
From talk of battles loud and vain,
And brawling memories all too free
For such a wise humility
As befits a solemn fane :
We revere, and while we hear
The tides of Music's golden sea
Setting toward eternity,
Uplifted high in heart and hope are we,
Until we doubt not that for one so true
There must be other nobler work to do
Than when he fought at Waterloo,
And Victor he must ever be.
For though the Giant Ages heave the hill
And break the shore, and evermore
Make and break, and work their will ;
Though world on world in myriad myriads roll
Round us, each with different powers,
And other forms of life than ours,
What know we greater than the soul ?
On God and godlike men we build our trust.
Hush, the Dead March wails in the people's ears :
The dark crowd moves, and there are sobs and tears :
The black earth yawns : the mortal disappears ;
Ashes to ashes, dust to dust ;
He is gone who seem'd so great.—

Gone ; but nothing can bereave him
Of the force he made his own
Being here, and we believe him
Something far advanced in State,
And that he wears a truer crown
Than any wreath that man can weave him.
But speak no more of his renown,
Lay your earthly fancies down,
And in the vast cathedral leave him,
God accept him, Christ receive him.

LORD TENNYSON.

NATIONALITY IN DRINKS

(EXTRACT.)

HERE's to Nelson's memory !
'Tis the second time that I, at sea,
Right off Cape Trafalgar here,
Have drunk it deep in British Beer.
Nelson for ever—any time
Am I his to command in prose or rhyme !
Give me of Nelson only a touch,
And I save it, be it little or much :
Here's one our Captain gives, and so
Down at the word, by George, shall it go !
He says that at Greenwich they point the beholder
To Nelson's coat " still with tar on the shoulder,
For he used to lean with one shoulder digging,
Jigging, as it were, and zig-zag-zigging
Up against the mizen-rigging ! "

ROBERT BROWNING.

PART III
POEMS OF ART

ANDREA DEL SARTO

(CALLED " THE FAULTLESS PAINTER ")

BUT do not let us quarrel any more,
No, my Lucrezia ; bear with me for once :
Sit down and all shall happen as you wish.
You turn your face, but does it bring your heart ?
I'll work then for your friend's friend, never fear,
Treat his own subject after his own way,
Fix his own time, accept too his own price,
And shut the money into this small hand
When next it takes mine.   Will it ? tenderly ?
Oh, I'll content him,—but to-morrow, love !
I often am much wearier than you think,
This evening more than usual, and it seems
As if—forgive now—should you let me sit
Here by the window with your hand in mine
And look a half-hour forth on Fiesole,
Both of one mind, as married people use,
Quietly, quietly the evening through,
I might get up to-morrow to my work
Cheerful and fresh as ever.   Let us try.
To-morrow, how you shall be glad for this !
Your soft hand is a woman of itself,
And mine the man's bared breast she curls inside.
Don't count the time lost, neither ; you must serve
For each of the five pictures we require :

It saves a model. So ! keep looking so—
My serpentining beauty, rounds on rounds !
—How could you ever prick those perfect ears,
Even to put the pearl there ! oh, so sweet—
My face, my moon, my everybody's moon,
Which everybody looks on and calls his,
And, I suppose, is looked on by in turn,
While she looks—no one's : very dear, no less.
You smile ? why, there's my picture ready made,
There's what we painters call our harmony !
A common greyness silvers everything,—
All in a twilight, you and I alike
—You, at the point of your first pride in me
(That's gone you know),—but I, at every point ;
My youth, my hope, my art, being all toned down
To yonder sober pleasant Fiesole.
There's the bell clinking from the chapel-top ;
That length of convent-wall across the way
Holds the trees safer, huddled more inside ;
The last monk leaves the garden ; days decrease.
And autumn grows, autumn in everything.
Eh ? the whole seems to fall into a shape
As if I saw alike my work and self
And all that I was born to be and do,
A twilight piece. Love, we are in God's hand.
How strange now, looks the life he makes us lead ;
So free we seem, so fettered fast we are !
I feel he laid the fetter ; let it lie !
This chamber for example—turn your head—
All that's behind us ! You don't understand
Nor care to understand about my art,
But you can hear at least when people speak :
And that cartoon, the second from the door
—It is the thing, love ! so such things should be—
Behold Madonna !—I am bold to say.
I can do with my pencil what I know,
What I see, what at bottom of my heart
I wish for, if I ever wish so deep—

Do easily, too—when I say, perfectly,
I do not boast, perhaps : yourself are judge
Who listened to the Legate's talk last week,
And just as much they used to say in France.
At any rate 'tis easy, all of it ;
No sketches first, no studies, that's long past :
I do what many dream of all their lives
—Dream ? strive to do, and agonize to do,
And fail in doing. I could count twenty such
On twice your fingers, and not leave this town,
Who strive—you don't know how the others strive
To paint a little thing like that you smeared
Carelessly passing with your robes afloat,—
Yet do much less, so much less, Someone says,
(I know his name, no matter)—so much less !
Well, less is more, Lucrezia : I am judged.
There burns a truer light of God in them,
In their vexed beating stuffed and stopped-up brain,
Heart, or whate'er else, than goes on to prompt
This low-pulsed forthright craftsman's hand of mine.
Their works drop groundward, but themselves, I know,
Reach many a time a heaven that's shut to me,
Enter and take their place there sure enough,
Though they come back and cannot tell the world.
My works are nearer heaven, but I sit here.
The sudden blood of these men ! at a word—
Praise them, it boils, or blame them, it boils too.
I, painting from myself and to myself,
Know what I do, am unmoved by men's blame
Or their praise either. Somebody remarks
Morello's outline there is wrongly traced,
His hue mistaken ; what of that ? or else,
Rightly traced and well ordered ; what of that ?
Speak as they please, what does the mountain care ?
Ah, but a man's reach should exceed his grasp,
Or what's a heaven for ? All is silver-grey
Placid and perfect with my art : the worse !
I know both what I want and what might gain ;

And yet how profitless to know, to sigh
" Had I been two, another and myself,
Our head would have overlooked the world ! "   No
     doubt.
Yonder's a work now, of that famous youth
The Urbinate who died five years ago.
('Tis copied, George Vasari sent it me.)
Well, I can fancy how he did it all,
Pouring his soul, with kings and popes to see,
Reaching, that heaven might so replenish him,
Above and through his art—for it gives way ;
That arm is wrongly put—and there again—
A fault to pardon in the drawing's lines,
Its body, so to speak : its soul is right,
He means right—that, a child may understand.
Still, what an arm ! and I could alter it :
But all the play, the insight and the stretch—
Out of me, out of me !   And wherefore out ?
Had you enjoined them on me, given me soul,
We might have risen to Rafael, I and you.
Nay, love, you did give all I asked, I think—
More than I merit, yes, by many times.
But had you—oh, with the same perfect brow,
And perfect eyes, and more than perfect mouth,
And the low voice my soul hears, as a bird
The fowler's pipe, and follows to the snare—
Had you, with these the same, but brought a mind !
Some women do so.   Had the mouth there urged
" God and the glory ! never care for gain.
The present by the future, what is that ?
Live for fame, side by side with Agnolo !
Rafael is waiting : up to God, all three ! "
I might have done it for you.   So it seems :
Perhaps not.   All is as God over-rules.
Beside, incentives come from the soul's self ;
The rest avail not.   Why do I need you ?
What wife had Rafael, or has Agnolo ?
In this world, who can do a thing, will not ;

And who would do it, cannot, I perceive :
Yet the will's somewhat—somewhat, too, the power—
And thus we half-men struggle.   At the end,
God, I conclude, compensates, punishes.
'Tis safer for me, if the award be strict,
That I am something underrated here,
Poor this long while, despised, to speak the truth.
I dared not, do you know, leave home all day,
For fear of chancing on the Paris lords.
The best is when they pass and look aside ;
But they speak sometimes ; I must bear it all.
Well may they speak ! That Francis, that first time,
And that long festal year at Fontainebleau !
I surely then could sometimes leave the ground,
Put on the glory, Rafael's daily wear,
In that humane great monarch's golden look,—
One finger in his beard or twisted curl
Over his mouth's good mark that made the smile,
One arm about my shoulder, round my neck,
The jingle of his gold chain in my ear,
I painting proudly with his breath on me,
All his court round him, seeing with his eyes,
Such frank French eyes, and such a fire of souls,
Profuse, my hand kept plying by those hearts,—
And, best of all, this, this, this face beyond,
This in the background, waiting on my work,
To crown the issue with a last reward !
A good time, was it not, my kingly days ?
And had you not grown restless . . . but I know—
'Tis done and past ; 'twas right, my instinct said :
Too live the life grew, golden and not grey,
And I'm the weak-eyed bat no sun should tempt
Out of the grange whose four walls make his world.
How could it end in any other way ?
You called me, and I came home to your heart.
The triumph was, to have ended there ; then, if
I reached it ere the triumph, what is lost ?
Let my hands frame your face in your hair's gold,

You beautiful Lucrezia that are mine !
" Rafael did this, Andrea painted that ;
The Roman's is the better when you pray,
But still the other's Virgin was his wife—"
Men will excuse me.   I am glad to judge
Both pictures in your presence ; clearer grows
My better fortune, I resolve to think.
For, do you know, Lucrezia, as God lives,
Said one day Agnolo, his very self,
To Rafael . . . I have known it all these years . . .
(When the young man was flaming out his thoughts
Upon a palace-wall for Rome to see,
Too lifted up in heart because of it)
" Friend, there's a certain sorry little scrub
Goes up and down our Florence, none cares how,
Who, were he set to plan and execute
As you are, pricked on by your popes and kings,
Would bring the sweat unto that brow of yours ! "
To Rafael's !—And indeed the arm is wrong.
I hardly dare . . . yet, only you to see,
Give the chalk here—quick, thus the line should go !
Ay, but the soul ! he's Rafael ! rub it out !
Still, all I care for, if he spoke the truth,
(What he ? why, who but Michel Agnolo ?
Do you forget already words like those ?)—
If really there was such a chance, so lost,—
Is, whether you're—not grateful—but more pleased.
Well, let me think so.   And you smile indeed !
This hour has been an hour !   Another smile ?
If you would sit thus by me every night
I should work better, do you comprehend ?
I mean that I should earn more, give you more.
See, it is settled dusk now ; there's a star ;
Morello's gone, the watch-lights show the wall,
The cue-owls speak the name we call them by.
Come from the window, love,—come in, at last,
Inside the melancholy little house
We built to be so gay with.   God is just.

King Francis may forgive me : oft at nights
When I look up from painting, eyes tired out,
The walls become illumined, brick from brick
Distinct, instead of mortar, fierce bright gold,
That gold of his I did cement them with !
Let us but love each other. Must you go ?
That Cousin here again ? he waits outside ?
Must see you—you, and not with me ? Those loans ?
More gaming debts to pay ? you smiled for that ?
Well, let smiles buy me ! have you more to spend ?
While hand and eye and something of a heart
Are left me, work's my ware, and what's it worth ?
I'll pay my fancy. Only let me sit
The grey remainder of the evening out,
Idle, you call it, and muse perfectly
How I could paint, were I but back in France,
One picture, just one more—the Virgin's face,
Not yours this time ! I want you at my side
To hear them—that is, Michel Agnolo—
Judge all I do and tell you of its worth.
Will you ? To-morrow, satisfy your friend.
I take the subjects for his corridor,
Finish the portrait out of hand—there, there,
And throw him in another thing or two
If he demurs ; the whole should prove enough
To pay for this same Cousin's freak. Beside,
What's better and what's all I care about,
Get you the thirteen scudi for the ruff !
Love, does that please you ! Ah, but what does he,
The Cousin ! what does he to please you more ?

I am grown peaceful as old age to-night.
I regret little, I would change still less.
Since there my past life lies, why alter it ?
The very wrong to Francis ! it is true
I took his coin, was tempted and complied,
And built this house and sinned, and all is said.
My father and my mother died of want.

Well, had I riches of my own ? you see
How one gets rich ! Let each one bear his lot.
They were born poor, lived poor, and poor they died :
And I have laboured somewhat in my time
And not been paid profusely. Some good son
Paint my two hundred pictures—let him try !
No doubt, there's something strikes a balance. Yes,
You loved me quite enough, it seems to-night.
This must suffice me here. What would one have ?
In heaven, perhaps, new chances, one more chance—
Four great walls in the New Jerusalem
Meted on each side by the angel's reed,
For Leonard, Rafael, Agnolo and me
To cover—the three first without a wife,
While I have mine ! So—still they overcome
Because there's still Lucrezia,—as I choose.

Again the Cousin's whistle ! Go, my love.

ROBERT BROWNING.

THE PALACE OF ART

I BUILT my soul a lordly pleasure-house,
    Wherein at ease for aye to dwell.
I said, " O Soul, make merry and carouse,
    Dear soul, for all is well."

A huge crag-platform, smooth as burnish'd brass,
    I chose. The ranged ramparts bright
From level meadow-bases of deep grass
    Suddenly scaled the light.

Thereon I built it firm. Of ledge or shelf
    The rock rose clear, or winding stair.
My soul would live alone unto herself
    In her high palace there.

And " while the world runs round and round," I said,
  " Reign thou apart, a quiet king,
Still as, while Saturn whirls, his steadfast shade
    Sleeps on his luminous ring."

To which my soul made answer readily :
  " Trust me, in bliss I shall abide
In this great mansion, that is built for me,
    So royal-rich and wide."

   *   *   *   *   *

Four courts I made, East, West, and South and North,
  In each a squared lawn, wherefrom
The golden gorge of dragons spouted forth
    A flood of fountain-foam.

And round the cool green courts there ran a row
  Of cloisters, branched like mighty woods,
Echoing all night to that sonorous flow
    Of spouted fountain-floods.

And round the roofs a gilded gallery
  That lent broad verge to distant lands,
Far as the wild swan wings, to where the sky
    Dipt down to sea and sands.

From those four jets four currents in one swell
  Across the mountain stream'd below
In misty folds, that floating as they fell
    Lit up a torrent-bow.

And high on every peak a statue seem'd
  To hang on tiptoe, tossing up
A cloud of incense of all odour steam'd
    From out a golden cup.

So that she thought, " And who shall gaze upon
  My palace with unblinded eyes,
While this great bow will waver in the sun,
    And that sweet incense rise ? "

For that sweet incense rose and never fail'd,
  And, while day sank or mounted higher,
The light aërial gallery, golden-rail'd,
  Burnt like a fringe of fire.

Likewise the deep-set windows, stain'd and traced,
  Would seem slow-flaming crimson fires
From shadow'd grots of arches interlaced,
  And tipt with frost-like spires.

            *   *   *   *   *

Full of long-sounding corridors it was,
  That over-vaulted grateful gloom,
Through which the livelong day my soul did pass,
  Well-pleased, from room to room.

Full of great rooms and small the palace stood,
  All various, each a perfect whole
From living Nature, fit for every mood
  And change of my still soul.

For some were hung with arras green and blue,
  Showing a gaudy summer-morn,
Where with puff'd cheek the belted hunter blew
  His wreathed bugle-horn.

One seem'd all dark and red—a tract of sand,
  And some one pacing there alone,
Who paced for ever in a glimmering land,
  Lit with a low large moon.

One show'd an iron coast and angry waves,
  You seem'd to hear them climb and fall
And roar rock-thwarted under bellowing caves
  Beneath the windy wall.

And one, a full-fed river winding slow
  By herds upon an endless plain,
The ragged rims of thunder brooding low
  With shadow-streaks of rain.

And one, the reapers at their sultry toil.
    In front they bound the sheaves.   Behind
Were realms of upland, prodigal in oil,
    And hoary to the wind.

And one, a foreground black with stones and slags,
    Beyond, a line of heights, and higher
All barr'd with long white cloud the scornful crags,
    And highest, snow and fire.

And one, an English home—grey twilight pour'd
    On dewy pastures, dewy trees,
Softer than sleep—all things in order stored,
    A haunt of ancient Peace.

Nor these alone, but every landscape fair,
    As fit for every mood of mind,
Or gay, or grave, or sweet, or stern, was there,
    Not less than truth design'd.

    *   *   *   *   *

Or the maid-mother by a crucifix,
    In tracts of pasture sunny-warm,
Beneath branch-work of costly sardonyx
    Sat smiling, babe in arm.

Or in a clear-walled city on the sea,
    Near gilded organ-pipes, her hair
Wound with white roses, slept St. Cecily ;
    An angel look'd at her.

Or thronging all one porch of Paradise,
    A group of Houris bow'd to see
The dying Islamite, with hands and eyes
    That said, We wait for thee.

Or mythic Uther's deeply-wounded son
    In some fair space of sloping greens
Lay, dozing in the vale of Avalon,
    And watch'd by weeping queens.

Or hollowing one hand against his ear
    To list a footfall ere he saw
The wood-nymph, stay'd the Ausonian king to hear
    Of wisdom and of law.

Or over hills with peaky tops engrail'd,
    And many a tract of palm and rice,
The throne of Indian Cama slowly sail'd
    A summer fann'd with spice.

Or sweet Europa's mantle blew unclasp'd,
    From off her shoulder backward borne ;
From one hand droop'd a crocus ; one hand grasp'd
    The mild bull's golden horn.

Or else flush'd Ganymede, his rosy thigh
    Half-buried in the Eagle's down,
Sole as a flying star shot through the sky
    Above the pillar'd town.

Nor these alone : but every legend fair
    Which the supreme Caucasian mind
Carved out of Nature for itself, was there,
    Not less than life, design'd.

   *   *   *   *   *

Then in the towers I placed great bells that swung,
    Moved of themselves, with silver sound ;
And with choice paintings of wise men I hung
    The royal dais round.

For there was Milton like a seraph strong ;
    Beside him Shakespeare bland and mild ;
And there the world-worn Dante grasp'd his song,
    And somewhat grimly smiled.

And there the Ionian father of the rest :
    A million wrinkles carved his skin ;
A hundred winters snow'd upon his breast,
    From cheek and throat and chin.

Above, the fair hall-ceiling stately-set
    Many an arch high up did lift,
And angels rising and descending met
    With interchange of gift.

Below was all mosaic choicely plann'd
    With cycles of the human tale
Of this wide world, the times of every land
    So wrought, they will not fail.

The people here, a beast of burden slow,
    Toil'd onward, prick'd with goads and stings ;
Here play'd a tiger, rolling to and fro
    The heads and crowns of kings ;

Here rose an athlete, strong to break or bind
    All force in bonds that might endure ;
And here once more like some sick man declined,
    And trusted any cure.

But over these she trod : and those great bells
    Began to chime.   She took her throne :
She sat betwixt the shining Oriels,
    To sing her songs alone.

And through the topmost Oriels' colour'd flame
    Two godlike faces gazed below ;
Plato the wise, and large-brow'd Verulam,
    The first of those who know.

And all those names, that in their motion were
    Full-welling fountain-heads of change,
Betwixt the slender shafts were blazon'd fair
    In diverse raiment strange :

Through which the lights, rose, amber, emerald, blue,
    Flush'd in her temples and her eyes,
And from her lips, as morn from Memnon, drew
    Rivers of melodies.

No nightingale delighteth to prolong
    Her low preamble all alone,
More than my soul to hear her echo'd song
    Throb through the ribbed stone ;

Singing and murmuring in her feastful mirth,
    Joying to feel herself alive,
Lord over Nature, Lord of the visible earth,
    Lord of the senses five ;

Communing with herself : " All these are mine,
    And let the world have peace or wars,
'Tis one to me." She—when young night divine
    Crown'd dying day with stars,

Making sweet close of his delicious toils—
    Lit light in wreaths and anadems,
And pure quintessences of precious oils
    In hollow'd moons of gems,

To mimic heaven ; and clapt her hands and cried,
    " I marvel if my still delight
In this great house so royal-rich, and wide,
    Be flatter'd to the height.

" O all things fair to sate my various eyes !
    O shapes and hues that please me well !
O silent faces of the Great and Wise,
    My Gods, with whom I dwell !

" O God-like isolation which art mine,
    I can but count thee perfect gain,
What time I watch the darkening droves of swine
    That range on yonder plain.

" In filthy sloughs they roll a prurient skin,
    They graze and wallow, breed and sleep ;
And oft some brainless devil enters in,
    And drives them to the deep."

Then of the moral instinct would she prate,
    And of the rising from the dead,
As hers by right of full-accomplish'd Fate ;
    And at the last she said :

" I take possession of man's mind and deed.
    I care not what the sects may brawl.
I sit as God holding no form of creed,
    But contemplating all."

    *   *   *   *   *

Full oft the riddle of the painful earth
    Flash'd through her as she sat alone,
Yet not the less held she her solemn mirth,
    And intellectual throne.

And so she throve and prosper'd : so three years
    She prosper'd : on the fourth she fell,
Like Herod, when the shout was in his ears,
    Struck through with pangs of hell.

Lest she should fail and perish utterly,
    God, before whom ever lie bare
The abysmal deeps of Personality,
    Plagued her with sore despair.

When she would think, where'er she turn'd her sight,
    The airy hand confusion wrought,
Wrote " Mene, mene," and divided quite
    The kingdom of her thought.

Deep dread and loathing of her solitude
    Fell on her, from which mood was born
Scorn of herself ; again, from out that mood
    Laughter at her self-scorn.

" What ! is not this my place of strength," she said,
    " My spacious mansion built for me,
Whereof the strong foundation-stones were laid
    Since my first memory ? "

But in dark corners of her palace stood
   Uncertain shapes ; and unawares
On white-eyed phantasms weeping tears of blood,
    And horrible nightmares,

And hollow shades enclosing hearts of flame,
   And, with dim fretted foreheads all,
On corpses three-months-old at noon she came,
    That stood against the wall.

A spot of dull stagnation, without light
   Or power of movement, seem'd my soul,
'Mid onward-sloping motions infinite
    Making for one sure goal.

A still salt pool, lock'd in with bars of sand ;
   Left on the shore ; that hears all night
The plunging seas draw backward from the land
    Their moon-led waters white.

A star that with the choral starry dance
   Join'd not, but stood, and standing saw
The hollow orb of moving Circumstance
    Roll'd round by one fix'd law.

Back on herself her serpent pride had curl'd.
   " No voice," she shriek'd in that lone hall,
" No voice breaks through the stillness of this world :
    One deep, deep silence all ! "

She, mouldering with the dull earth's mouldering sod,
   Inwrapt tenfold in slothful shame,
Lay there exiled from eternal God,
    Lost to her place and name ;

And death and life she hated equally,
   And nothing saw, for her despair,
But dreadful time, dreadful eternity,
    No comfort anywhere ;

(2,599)

Remaining utterly confused with fears,
   And ever worse with growing time,
And ever unrelieved by dismal tears,
   And all alone in crime :

Shut up as in a crumbling tomb, girt round
   With blackness as a solid wall,
Far off she seem'd to hear the dully sound
   Of human footsteps fall.

As in strange lands a traveller walking slow,
   In doubt and great perplexity,
A little before moon-rise hears the low
   Moan of an unknown sea ;

And knows not if it be thunder or a sound
   Of rocks thrown down, or one deep cry
Of great wild beasts ; then thinketh, " I have found
   A new land, but I die."

She howl'd aloud, " I am on fire within.
   There comes no murmur of reply.
What is it that will take away my sin,
   And save me lest I die ? "

So when four years were wholly finished,
   She threw her royal robes away.
" Make me a cottage in the vale," she said,
   " Where I may mourn and pray.

" Yet pull not down my palace towers, that are
   So lightly, beautifully built :
Perchance I may return with others there
   When I have purged my guilt."

LORD TENNYSON.

FRA LIPPO LIPPI

I AM poor brother Lippo, by your leave !
You need not clap your torches to my face.
Zooks, what's to blame ? you think you see a monk !
What, 'tis past midnight, and you go the rounds,
And here you catch me at an alley's end
Where sportive ladies leave their doors ajar ?
The Carmine's my cloister : hunt it up,
Do,—harry out, if you must show your zeal,
Whatever rat, there, haps on his wrong hole,
And nip each softling of a wee white mouse,
Weke, weke, that's crept to keep him company !
Aha, you know your betters ? Then, you'll take
Your hand away that's fiddling on my throat,
And please to know me likewise. Who am I ?
Why, one, sir, who is lodging with a friend
Three streets off—he's a certain . . . how d'ye call ?
Master—a . . . Cosimo of the Medici,
In the house that caps the corner. Boh ! you were
            best !
Remember and tell me, the day you're hanged,
How you affected such a gullet's-gripe !
But you, sir, it concerns you that your knaves
Pick up a manner nor discredit you :
Zooks, are we pilchards, that they sweep the streets
And count fair prize what comes into their net ?
He's Judas to a tittle, that man is !
Just such a face ! Why, sir, you make amends.
Lord, I'm not angry ! Bid your hangdogs go
Drink out this quarter-florin to the health
Of the munificent House that harbours me
(And many more beside, lads ! more beside !)
And all's come square again. I'd like his face—
His, elbowing on his comrade in the door
With the pike and lantern,—for the slave that holds

John Baptist's head a-dangle by the hair
With one hand (" Look you, now," as who should say)
And his weapon in the other, yet unwiped !
It's not your chance to have a bit of chalk,
A wood-coal or the like ? or you should see !
Yes, I'm the painter, since you style me so.
What, brother Lippo's doings, up and down,
You know them and they take you ? like enough !
I saw the proper twinkle in your eye—
'Tell you, I liked your looks at very first.
Let's sit and set things straight now, hip to haunch.
Here's spring come, and the nights one makes up bands
To roam the town and sing out carnival,
And I've been three weeks shut within my mew,
A-painting for the great man, saints and saints
And saints again. I could not paint all night—
Ouf ! I leaned out of window for fresh air.
There came a hurry of feet and little feet,
A sweep of lute-strings, laughs, and whiffs of song,—
Flower o' the broom,
Take away love, and our earth is a tomb !
Flower o' the quince,
I let Lisa go, and what good in life since ?
Flower o' the thyme—and so on. Round they went.
Scarce had they turned the corner when a titter
Like the skipping of rabbits by moonlight,—three
    slim shapes,
And a face that looked up . . . zooks, sir, flesh and
    blood,
That's all I'm made of ! Into shreds it went,
Curtain and counterpane and coverlet,
All the bed-furniture—a dozen knots,
There was a ladder ! Down I let myself,
Hands and feet, scrambling somehow, and so dropped,
And after them. I came up with the fun
Hard by Saint Laurence, hail fellow, well met,—
Flower o' the rose,
If I've been merry, what matter who knows ?

And so as I was stealing back again
To get to bed and have a bit of sleep
Ere I rise up to-morrow and go work
On Jerome knocking at his poor old breast
With his great round stone to subdue the flesh,
You snap me of the sudden. Ah, I see !
Though your eye twinkles still, you shake your head—
Mine's shaved—a monk, you say—the sting's in that !
If Master Cosimo announced himself,
Mum's the word naturally ; but a monk !
Come, what am I a beast for ? tell us, now !
I was a baby when my mother died
And father died and left me in the street.
I starved there, God knows how, a year or two
On fig-skins, melon-parings, rinds and shucks,
Refuse and rubbish. One fine frosty day,
My stomach being empty as your hat,
The wind doubled me up and down I went.
Old Aunt Lapaccia trussed me with one hand,
(Its fellow was a stinger as I knew)
And so along the wall, over the bridge,
By the straight cut to the convent. Six words there,
While I stood munching my first bread that month :
" So, boy, you're minded," quoth the good fat father,
Wiping his own mouth, 'twas refection-time,—
" To quit this very miserable world ?
Will you renounce " . . . " the mouthful of bread ? "
      thought I ;
By no means ! Brief, they made a monk of me ;
I did renounce the world, its pride and greed,
Palace, farm, villa, shop and banking-house,
Trash, such as these poor devils of Medici
Have given their hearts to—all at eight years old.
Well, sir, I found in time, you may be sure,
'Twas not for nothing—the good bellyful,
The warm serge and the rope that goes all round,
And day-long blessed idleness beside !
." Let's see what the urchin's fit for "—that came next.

Not overmuch their way, I must confess.
Such a to-do! They tried me with their books:
Lord, they'd have taught me Latin in pure waste!
Flower o' the clove,
All the Latin I construe is, " amo " I love!
But, mind you, when a boy starves in the streets
Eight years together as my fortune was,
Watching folk's faces to know who will fling
The bit of half-stripped grape-bunch he desires,
And who will curse or kick him for his pains,—
Which gentleman processional and fine,
Holding a candle to the Sacrament
Will wink and let him lift a plate and catch
The droppings of the wax to sell again,
Or holla for the Eight and have him whipped,—
How say I?—nay, which dog bites, which lets drop
His bone from the heap of offal in the street,—
Why, soul and sense of him grow sharp alike,
He learns the look of things, and none the less
For admonition from the hunger-pinch.
I had a store of such remarks, be sure,
Which, after I found leisure, turned to use:
I drew men's faces on my copy-books,
Scrawled them within the antiphonary's marge,
Joined legs and arms to the long music-notes,
Found eyes and nose and chin for A's and B's,
And made a string of pictures of the world
Betwixt the ins and outs of verb and noun,
On the wall, the bench, the door. The monks looked
    black.
" Nay," quoth the Prior, " turn him out, d'ye say?
In no wise. Lose a crow and catch a lark.
What if at last we get our man of parts,
We Carmelites, like those Camaldolese
And Preaching Friars, to do our church up fine
And put the front on it that ought to be!"
And hereupon he bade me daub away.
Thank you! my head being crammed, the walls a blank,

Never was such prompt disemburdening.
First, every sort of monk, the black and white,
I drew them, fat and lean : then, folks at church,
From good old gossips waiting to confess
Their cribs of barrel-droppings, candle-ends,—
To the breathless fellow at the altar-foot,
Fresh from his murder, safe and sitting there
With the little children round him in a row
Of admiration, half for his beard and half
For that white anger of his victim's son
Shaking a fist at him with one fierce arm,
Signing himself with the other because of Christ
(Whose sad face on the cross sees only this
After the passion of a thousand years)
Till some poor girl, her apron o'er her head,
(Which the intense eyes looked through) came at eve
On tip-toe, said a word, dropped in a loaf,
Her pair of earrings and a bunch of flowers
(The brute took growling) prayed, and so was gone.
I painted all, then cried " 'Tis ask and have ;
Choose, for more's ready ! "—laid the ladder flat,
And showed my covered bit of cloister-wall.
The monks closed in a circle and praised loud
Till checked, taught what to see and not to see,
Being simple bodies,—" That's the very man !
Look at the boy who stoops to pat the dog !
That woman's like the Prior's niece who comes
To care about his asthma : it's the life ! "
But there my triumph's straw-fire flared and funked ;
Their betters took their turn to see and say :
The Prior and the learned pulled a face
And stopped all that in no time. " How ? what's
      here ?
Quite from the mark of painting, bless us all !
Faces, arms, legs and bodies like the true
As much as pea and pea ! it's devil's game !
Your business is not to catch men with show,
With homage to the perishable clay,

But lift them over it, ignore it all,
Make them forget there's such a thing as flesh.
Your business is to paint the souls of men—
Man's soul, and it's a fire, smoke . . . no, it's not . . .
It's vapour done up like a new-born babe—
(In that shape when you die it leaves your mouth)
It's . . . well, what matters talking, it's the soul !
Give us no more of body than shows soul !
Here's Giotto, with his Saint a-praising God,
That sets us praising,—why not stop with him ?
Why put all thoughts of praise out of our head
With wonder at lines, colours, and what not ?
Paint the soul, never mind the legs and arms !
Rub all out, try at it a second time.
Oh, that white smallish female with the breasts,
She's just my niece . . . Herodias, I would say,—
Who went and danced and got men's heads cut off !
Have it all out ! ''   Now, is this sense, I ask ?
A fine way to paint soul, by painting body
So ill, the eye can't stop there, must go further
And can't fare worse !   Thus, yellow does for white
When what you put for yellow's simply black,
And any sort of meaning looks intense
When all beside itself means and looks nought.
Why can't a painter lift each foot in turn,
Left foot and right foot, go a double step,
Make his flesh liker and his soul more like,
Both in their order ?   Take the prettiest face,
The Prior's niece . . . patron-saint—is it so pretty
You can't discover if it means hope, fear,
Sorrow or joy ?   won't beauty go with these ?
Suppose I've made her eyes all right and blue,
Can't I take breath and try to add life's flash,
And then add soul and heighten them threefold ?
Or say there's beauty with no soul at all—
(I never saw it—put the case the same—)
If you get simple beauty and nought else,
You get about the best thing God invents :

That's somewhat : and you'll find the soul you have
    missed,
Within yourself, when you return him thanks.
" Rub all out ! " Well, well, there's my life, in short ;
And so the thing has gone on ever since.
I'm grown a man no doubt, I've broken bounds :
You should not take a fellow eight years old
And make him swear to never kiss the girls.
I'm my own master, paint now as I please—
Having a friend, you see, in the Corner-house !
Lord, it's fast holding by the rings in front—
Those great rings serve more purposes than just
To plant a flag in, or tie up a horse !
And yet the old schooling sticks, the old grave eyes
Are peeping o'er my shoulder as I work,
The heads shake still—" It's art's decline, my son !
You're not of the true painters, great and old ;
Brother Angelico's the man, you'll find ;
Brother Lorenzo stands his single peer :
Fag on at flesh, you'll never make the third ! "
Flower o' the pine,
You keep your mistr . . . manners, and I'll stick to
    mine !
I'm not the third, then : bless us, they must know !
Don't you think they're the likeliest to know,
They with their Latin ? So, I swallow my rage,
Clench my teeth, suck my lips in tight, and paint
To please them—sometimes do, and sometimes don't ;
For, doing most, there's pretty sure to come
A turn, some warm eve finds me at my saints—
A laugh, a cry, the business of the world—
(*Flower o' the peach,*
Death for us all, and his own life for each !)
And my whole soul revolves, the cup runs over,
The world and life's too big to pass for a dream,
And I do these wild things in sheer despite,
And play the fooleries you catch me at,
In pure rage ! The old mill-horse, out at grass

After hard years, throws up his stiff heels so,
Although the miller does not preach to him
The only good of grass is to make chaff.
What would men have ? Do they like grass or no—
May they or mayn't they ? all I want's the thing
Settled for ever one way. As it is,
You tell too many lies and hurt yourself ;
You don't like what you only like too much,
You do like what, if given you at your word,
You find abundantly detestable.
For me, I think I speak as I was taught ;
I always see the garden and God there
A-making man's wife : and, my lesson learned,
The value and significance of flesh,
I can't unlearn ten minutes afterwards.

You understand me : I'm a beast, I know.
But see, now—why, I see as certainly
As that the morning-star's about to shine,
What will hap some day. We've a youngster here
Comes to our convent, studies what I do,
Slouches and stares and lets no atom drop :
His name is Guidi—he'll not mind the monks—
They call him Hulking Tom, he lets them talk—
He picks my practice up—he'll paint apace,
I hope so—though I never live so long,
I know what's sure to follow. You be judge !
You speak no Latin more than I, belike ;
However, you're my man, you've seen the world
—The beauty and the wonder and the power,
The shapes of things, their colours, light and shades,
Changes, surprises,—and God made it all !
—For what ? Do you feel thankful, ay or no.
For this fair town's face, yonder river's line,
The mountain round it and the sky above,
Much more the figures of man, woman, child,
These are the frame to ? What's it all about ?
To be passed over, despised ? or dwelt upon,

Wondered at ? oh, this last of course !—you say.
But why not do as well as say,—paint these
Just as they are, careless what comes of it ?
God's works—paint any one, and count it crime
To let a truth slip. Don't object, " His works
Are here already ; nature is complete :
Suppose you reproduce her—(which you can't)
There's no advantage ! you must beat her, then."
For, don't you mark, we're made so that we love
First when we see them painted, things we have passed
Perhaps a hundred times nor cared to see ;
And so they are better, painted—better to us,
Which is the same thing. Art was given for that ;
God uses us to help each other so,
Lending our minds out. Have you noticed, now,
Your cullion's hanging face ? A bit of chalk,
And trust me but you should, though ! How much
  more,
If I drew higher things with the same truth !
That were to take the Prior's pulpit-place,
Interpret God to all of you ! Oh, oh,
It makes me mad to see what men shall do
And we in our graves ! This world's no blot for us,
Nor blank ; it means intensely, and means good ;
To find its meaning is my meat and drink.
" Ay, but you don't so instigate to prayer ! "
Strikes in the Prior : " when your meaning's plain
It does not say to folks—remember matins,
Or, mind you fast next Friday ! " Why, for this
What need of art at all ? A skull and bones,
Two bits of stick nailed cross-wise, or, what's best,
A bell to chime the hour with, does as well.
I painted a Saint Laurence six months since
At Prato, splashed the fresco in fine style :
" How looks my painting, now the scaffold's down ? "
I ask a brother : " Hugely," he returns—
" Already not one phiz of your three slaves
Who turn the Deacon off his toasted side,

But's scratched and prodded to our heart's content,
The pious people have so eased their own
With coming to say prayers there in a rage :
We get on fast to see the bricks beneath.
Expect another job this time next year,
For pity and religion grow i' the crowd—
Your painting serves its purpose ! " Hang the fools !

—That is—you'll not mistake an idle word
Spoke in a huff by a poor monk, God wot,
Tasting the air this spicy night which turns
The unaccustomed head like Chianti wine !
Oh, the church knows ! don't misreport me, now !
It's natural a poor monk out of bounds
Should have his apt word to excuse himself :
And hearken how I plot to make amends.
I have bethought me : I shall paint a piece
. . . There's for you ! Give me six months, then go, see
Something in Sant' Ambrogio's ! Bless the nuns !
They want a cast of my office. I shall paint
God in the midst, Madonna and her babe,
Ringed by a bowery, flowery angel-brood,
Lilies and vestments and white faces, sweet
As puff on puff of grated orris-root
When ladies crowd to church at midsummer.
And then in the front, of course a saint or two—
Saint John, because he saves the Florentines,
Saint Ambrose, who puts down in black and white
The convent's friends and gives them a long day,
And Job, I must have him there past mistake,
The man of Uz, (and Us without the z,
Painters who need his patience.) Well, all these
Secured at their devotion, up shall come
Out of a corner when you least expect,
As one by a dark stair into a great light,
Music and talking, who but Lippo ! I !—
Mazed, motionless and moonstruck—I'm the man !
Back I shrink—what is this I see and hear ?

I, caught up with my monk's things by mistake,
My old serge gown and rope that goes all round,
I, in this presence, this pure company !
Where's a hole, where's a corner for escape ?
Then steps a sweet angelic slip of a thing
Forward, puts out a soft palm—" Not so fast ! "
—Addresses the celestial presence, " nay—
He made you and devised you, after all,
Though he's none of you ! Could Saint John there,
    draw—
His camel-hair make up a painting-brush ?
We come to brother Lippo for all that,
Iste perfecit opus ! " So, all smile—
I shuffle sideways with my blushing face
Under the cover of a hundred wings
Thrown like a spread of kirtles when you're gay
And play hot cockles, all the doors being shut,
Till, wholly unexpected, in there pops
The hothead husband ! Thus I scuttle off
To some safe bench behind, not letting go
The palm of her, the little lily thing
That spoke the good word for me in the nick,
Like the Prior's niece . . . Saint Lucy, I would say.
And so all's saved for me, and for the church
A pretty picture gained. Go, six months hence !
Your hand, sir, and good bye : no lights, no lights !
The street's hushed, and I know my own way back,
Don't fear me ! There's the grey beginning. Zooks !

                        ROBERT BROWNING.

PART IV

POEMS OF LOVE

GARDEN FANCIES

THE FLOWER'S NAME

HERE's the garden she walked across,
  Arm in my arm, such a short while since :
Hark, now I push its wicket, the moss
  Hinders the hinges and makes them wince !
She must have reached this shrub ere she turned,
  As back with that murmur the wicket swung ;
For she laid the poor snail, my chance foot spurned,
  To feed and forget it the leaves among.

Down this side of the gravel-walk
  She went while her robe's edge brushed the box :
And here she paused in her gracious talk
  To point me a moth on the milk-white phlox.
Roses, ranged in valiant row,
  I will never think that she passed you by !
She loves you noble roses, I know ;
  But yonder, see, where the rock-plants lie !

This flower she stopped at, finger on lip,
  Stooped over, in doubt, as settling its claim ;
Till she gave me, with pride to make no slip,
  Its soft meandering Spanish name ;
What a name ! Was it love or praise ?
  Speech half-asleep or song half-awake ?

I must learn Spanish, one of these days,
    Only for that slow sweet name's sake.

Roses, if I live and do well,
    I may bring her, one of these days,
To fix you fast with as fine a spell,
    Fit you each with his Spanish phrase ;
But do not detain me now ; for she lingers
    There, like sunshine over the ground,
And ever I see her soft white fingers
    Searching after the bud she found.

Flower, you Spaniard, look that you grow not,
    Stay as you are and be loved for ever !
Bud, if I kiss you 'tis that you blow not,
    Mind, the shut pink mouth opens never !
For while it pouts, her fingers wrestle,
    Twinkling the audacious leaves between,
Till round they turn and down they nestle—
    Is not the dear mark still to be seen ?

Where I find her not, beauties vanish ;
    Whither I follow her, beauties flee ;
Is there no method to tell her in Spanish
    June's twice June since she breathed it with me ?
Come, bud, show me the least of her traces,
    Treasure my lady's lightest footfall !
—Ah, you may flout and turn up your faces—
    Roses, you are not so fair after all !

                                    ROBERT BROWNING.

SONG

NAY but you, who do not love her,
    Is she not pure gold, my mistress ?
Holds earth aught—speak truth—above her ?
    Aught like this tress, see, and this tress,

And this last fairest tress of all,
So fair, see, ere I let it fall ?

Because, you spend your lives in praising ;
    To praise, you search the wide world over :
Then why not witness, calmly gazing,
    If earth holds aught—speak truth—above her ?
Above this tress, and this, I touch
But cannot praise, I love so much !

ROBERT BROWNING.

ONE WAY OF LOVE

ALL June I bound the rose in sheaves.
Now, rose by rose, I strip the leaves
And strew them where Pauline may pass.
She will not turn aside ? Alas !
Let them lie. Suppose they die ?
The chance was they might take her eye.

How many a month I strove to suit
These stubborn fingers to the lute !
To-day I venture all I know.
She will not hear my music ? So !
Break the string ; fold music's wing :
Suppose Pauline had bade me sing !

My whole life long I learned to love.
This hour my utmost art I prove
And speak my passion—heaven or hell ?
She will not give me heaven ? 'Tis well !
Lose who may—I still can say,
Those who win heaven, blest are they !

ROBERT BROWNING.

ANOTHER WAY OF LOVE

JUNE was not over
   Though past the full,
And the best of her roses
   Had yet to blow,
   When a man I know
(But shall not discover,
   Since ears are dull,
And time discloses)
Turned him and said with a man's true air,
Half sighing a smile in a yawn, as 'twere,—
" If I tire of your June, will she greatly care ? "

Well, dear, in-doors with you !
   True ! serene deadness
Tries a man's temper.
   What's in the blossom
   June wears on her bosom ?
Can it clear scores with you ?
   Sweetness and redness,
   Eadem semper !
Go, let me care for it greatly or slightly !
If June mend her bower now, your hand left unsightly
By plucking the roses,—my June will do rightly.

And after, for pastime,
   If June be refulgent
With flowers in completeness,
   All petals, no prickles,
   Delicious as trickles
Of wine poured at mass-time,—
   And choose One indulgent
   To redness and sweetness :
   (2,599)

Or if, with experience of man and of spider,
June use my June-lightning, the strong insect-ridder,
And stop the fresh film-work,—why, June will consider.

ROBERT BROWNING.

EXTRACTS FROM MAUD

I

[The speaker is in love with Maud, whom, for family
and financial reasons, he cannot marry. Her father and
brother wish her to marry the " young Lord-lover," but
she returns the speaker's affection, and goes to meet him
in the garden after a dance. Her brother finds them
together, and a duel takes place, in which the brother is
shot. The speaker flies abroad, to brood over the past.]

I

BIRDS in the high Hall-garden
    When twilight was falling,
Maud, Maud, Maud, Maud,
    They were crying and calling.

II

Where was Maud ? in our wood ;
    And I, who else, was with her,
Gathering woodland lilies,
    Myriads blow together.

III

Birds in our wood sang
    Ringing through the valleys,
Maud is here, here, here,
    In among the lilies.

IV

I kiss'd her slender hand,
    She took the kiss sedately ;
Maud is not seventeen,
    But she is tall and stately.

V

I to cry out on pride
　　Who have won her favour !
Oh, Maud were sure of Heaven
　　If lowliness could save her.

VI

I know the way she went
　　Home with her maiden posy,
For her feet have touch'd the meadows,
　　And left the daisies rosy.

VII

Birds in the high Hall-garden
　　Were crying and calling to her,
Where is Maud, Maud, Maud ?
　　One is come to woo her.

VIII

Look, a horse at the door,
　　And little King Charles is snarling,
Go back, my lord, across the moor,
　　You are not her darling.

II

Go not, happy day,
　　From the shining fields,
Go not, happy day,
　　Till the maiden yields.
Rosy is the West,
　　Rosy is the South,
Roses are her cheeks,
　　And a rose her mouth.

When the happy Yes
  Falters from her lips,
Pass and blush the news
  O'er the blowing ships ;
Over blowing seas,
  Over seas at rest,
Pass the happy news,
  Blush it through the West ;
Till the red man dance
  By his red cedar tree,
And the red man's babe
  Leap, beyond the sea.
Blush from West to East,
  Blush from East to West,
Till the West is East,
  Blush it through the West.
Rosy is the West,
  Rosy is the South,
Roses are her cheeks,
  And a rose her mouth.

III

I

A VOICE by the cedar tree,
In the meadow under the Hall !
She is singing an air that is known to me,
A passionate ballad gallant and gay,
A martial song like a trumpet's call !
Singing alone in the morning of life,
In the happy morning of life and of May,
Singing of men that in battle array,
Ready in heart and ready in hand,
March with banner and bugle and fife
To the death, for their native land.

II

Maud with her exquisite face,
And wild voice pealing up to the sunny sky,
And feet like sunny gems on an English green,
Maud in the light of her youth and her grace,
Singing of Death, and of Honour that cannot die,
Till I well could weep for a time so sordid and mean,
And myself so languid and base.

III

Silence, beautiful voice !
Be still, for you only trouble the mind
With a joy in which I cannot rejoice,
A glory I shall not find.
Still ! I will hear you no more,
For your sweetness hardly leaves me a choice
But to move to the meadow and fall before
Her feet on the meadow grass, and adore,
Not her, who is neither courtly nor kind,
Not her, not her, but a voice.

IV

I

COME into the garden, Maud,
    For the black bat, night, has flown,
Come into the garden, Maud,
    I am here at the gate alone ;
And the woodbine spices are wafted abroad,
    And the musk of the roses blown.

II

For a breeze of morning moves,
    And the planet of Love is on high,

Beginning to faint in the light that she loves
    On a bed of daffodil sky,
To faint in the light of the sun she loves,
    To faint in his light, and to die.

III

All night have the roses heard
    The flute, violin, bassoon ;
All night has the casement jessamine stirr'd
    To the dancers dancing in tune ;
Till a silence fell with the waking bird,
    And a hush with the setting moon.

IV

I said to the lily, " There is but one
    With whom she has heart to be gay.
When will the dancers leave her alone ?
    She is weary of dance and play."
Now half to the setting moon are gone,
    And half to the rising day ;
Low on the sand and loud on the stone
    The last wheel echoes away.

V

I said to the rose, " The brief night goes
    In babble and revel and wine.
O young lord-lover, what sighs are those
    For one that will never be thine ?
But mine, but mine," so I sware to the rose,
    " For ever and ever, mine."

VI

And the soul of the rose went into my blood,
    As the music clash'd in the hall ;

And long by the garden lake I stood,
    For I heard your rivulet fall
From the lake to the meadow and on to the wood,
    Our wood that is dearer than all ;

VII

From the meadow your walks have left so sweet
    That whenever a March wind sighs
He sets the jewel-print of your feet
    In violets blue as your eyes,
To the woody hollows in which we meet
    And the valleys of Paradise.

VIII

The slender acacia would not shake
    One long milk-bloom on the tree ;
The white lake-blossom fell into the lake,
    As the pimpernel dozed on the lea ;
But the rose was awake all night for your sake,
    Knowing your promise to me ;
The lilies and roses were all awake,
    They sigh'd for the dawn and thee.

IX

Queen rose of the rosebud garden of girls,
    Come hither, the dances are done,
In gloss of satin and glimmer of pearls,
    Queen lily and rose in one ;
Shine out, little head, sunning over with curls,
    To the flowers, and be their sun.

X

There has fallen a splendid tear
    From the passion-flower at the gate.

She is coming, my dove, my dear ;
　She is coming, my life, my fate.
The red rose cries, " She is near, she is near ; "
　And the white rose weeps, " She is late ; "
The larkspur listens, " I hear, I hear ; "
　And the lily whispers, " I wait."

XI

She is coming, my own, my sweet ;
　Were it ever so airy a tread,
My heart would hear her and beat,
　Were it earth in an earthy bed ;
My dust would hear her and beat,
　Had I lain for a century dead ;
Would start and tremble under her feet,
　And blossom in purple and red.
LORD TENNYSON.

A WOMAN'S LAST WORD

LET's contend no more, Love,
　Strive nor weep :
All be as before, Love,
　—Only sleep !

What so wild as words are ?
　I and thou
In debate, as birds are,
　Hawk on bough !

See the creature stalking
　While we speak !
Hush and hide the talking,
　Cheek on cheek !

What so false as truth is,
　　False to thee ?
Where the serpent's tooth is,
　　Shun the tree—

Where the apple reddens
　　Never pry—
Lest we lose our Edens,
　　Eve and I.

Be a god and hold me
　　With a charm !
Be a man and fold me
　　With thine arm !

Teach me, only teach, Love !
　　As I ought
I will speak thy speech, Love,
　　Think thy thought—

Meet, if thou require it,
　　Both demands,
Laying flesh and spirit
　　In thy hands.

That shall be to-morrow
　　Not to-night :
I must bury sorrow
　　Out of sight :

—Must a little weep, Love,
　　(Foolish me !)
And so fall asleep, Love,
　　Loved by thee.

ROBERT BROWNING.

ANY WIFE TO ANY HUSBAND

My love, this is the bitterest, that thou—
Who art all truth, and who dost love me now
    As thine eyes say, as thy voice breaks to say—
Shouldst love so truly, and couldst love me still
A whole long life through, had but love its will,
    Would death that leads me from thee brook delay.

I have but to be by thee, and thy hand
Will never let mine go, nor heart withstand
    The beating of my heart to reach its place.
When shall I look for thee and feel thee gone ?
When cry for the old comfort and find none ?
    Never, I know ! Thy soul is in thy face.

Oh, I should fade—'tis willed so ! Might I save,
Gladly I would, whatever beauty gave
    Joy to thy sense, for that was precious too.
It is not to be granted. But the soul
Whence the love comes, all ravage leaves that whole ;
    Vainly the flesh fades ; soul makes all things new.

It would not be because my eye grew dim
Thou couldst not find the love there, thanks to Him
    Who never is dishonoured in the spark
He gave us from His fire of fires, and bade
Remember whence it sprang, nor be afraid
    While that burns on, though all the rest grow dark.

So, how thou wouldst be perfect, white and clean
Outside as inside, soul and soul's demesne
    Alike, this body given to show it by !
Oh, three-parts through the worst of life's abyss,
What plaudits from the next world after this,
    Couldst thou repeat a stroke and gain the sky !

And is it not the bitterer to think
That disengage our hands and thou wilt sink
   Although thy love was love in very deed ?
I know that nature !   Pass a festive day,
Thou dost not throw its relic-flower away
   Nor bid its music's loitering echo speed.

Thou let'st the stranger's glove lie where it fell ;
If old things remain old things all is well,
   For thou art grateful as becomes man best :
And hadst thou only heard me play one tune,
Or viewed me from a window, not so soon
   With thee would such things fade as with the rest.

I seem to see !   We meet and part ; 'tis brief ;
The book I opened keeps a folded leaf,
   The very chair I sat on, breaks the rank ;
That is a portrait of me on the wall—
Three lines, my face comes at so slight a call :
   And for all this, one little hour to thank !

But now, because the hour through years was fixed,
Because our inmost beings met and mixed,
   Because thou once hast loved me—wilt thou dare
Say to thy soul and Who may list beside,
" Therefore she is immortally my bride ;
   Chance cannot change my love, nor time impair.

" So, what if in the dusk of life that's left,
I, a tired traveller of my sun bereft,
   Look from my path when, mimicking the same,
The fire-fly glimpses past me, come and gone ?
—Where was it till the sunset ? where anon
   It will be at the sunrise !   What's to blame ? "

Is it so helpful to thee ?   Canst thou take
The mimic up, nor, for the true thing's sake,
   Put gently by such efforts at a beam ?

Is the remainder of the way so long
Thou need'st the little solace, thou the strong ?
    Watch out thy watch, let weak ones doze and dream !

—Ah, but the fresher faces ! " Is it true,"
Thou'lt ask, " some eyes are beautiful and new ?
    Some hair,—how can one choose but grasp such
        wealth ?
And if a man would press his lips to lips
Fresh as the wilding hedge-rose-cup there slips
    The dew-drop out of, must it be by stealth ?

" It cannot change the love still kept for Her,
More than if such a picture I prefer
    Passing a day with, to a room's bare side :
The painted form takes nothing she possessed,
Yet, while the Titian's Venus lies at rest,
    A man looks.   Once more, what is there to chide ? "

So I must see, from where I sit and watch,
My own self sell myself, my hand attach
    Its warrant to the very thefts from me—
Thy singleness of soul that made me proud,
Thy purity of heart I loved aloud,
    Thy man's-truth I was bold to bid God see !

Love so, then, if thou wilt !   Give all thou canst
Away to the new faces—disentranced,
    (Say it and think it) obdurate no more,
Re-issue looks and words from the old mint,
Pass them afresh, no matter whose the print
    Image and superscription once they bore !

Re-coin thyself and give it them to spend,—
It all comes to the same thing at the end,
    Since mine thou wast, mine art and mine shalt be,
Faithful or faithless, sealing up the sum
Or lavish of my treasure, thou must come
    Back to the heart's place here I keep for thee !

Only, why should it be with stain at all ?
Why must I, 'twixt the leaves of coronal,
  Put any kiss of pardon on thy brow ?
Why need the other women know so much,
And talk together, " Such the look and such
  The smile he used to love with, then as now ! "

Might I die last and show thee !   Should I find
Such hardship in the few years left behind,
  If free to take and light my lamp, and go
Into thy tomb, and shut the door and sit,
Seeing thy face on those four sides of it
  The better that they are so blank, I know !

Why, time was what I wanted, to turn o'er
Within my mind each look, get more and more
  By heart each word, too much to learn at first ;
And join thee all the fitter for the pause
'Neath the low door-way's lintel.   That were cause
  For lingering, though thou calledst, if I durst !

And yet thou art the nobler of us two :
What dare I dream of, that thou canst not do,
  Outstripping my ten small steps with one stride ?
I'll say then, here's a trial and a task—
Is it to bear ?—if easy, I'll not ask :
  Though love fail, I can trust on in thy pride.

Pride ?—when those eyes forestall the life behind
The death I have to go through !—when I find,
  Now that I want thy help most, all of thee !
What did I fear ?   Thy love shall hold me fast
Until the little minute's sleep is past
  And I wake saved.—And yet it will not be !

ROBERT BROWNING.

THE STATUE AND THE BUST

THERE'S a palace in Florence, the world knows well,
And a statue watches it from the square,
And this story of both do our townsmen tell.

Ages ago, a lady there,
At the farthest window facing the East
Asked, " Who rides by with the royal air ? "

The bridesmaids' prattle around her ceased ;
She leaned forth, one on either hand ;
They saw how the blush of the bride increased—

They felt by its beats her heart expand—
As one at each ear and both in a breath
Whispered, " The Great-Duke Ferdinand."

That selfsame instant, underneath,
The Duke rode past in his idle way,
Empty and fine like a swordless sheath.

Gay he rode, with a friend as gay,
Till he threw his head back—" Who is she ? "
—" A bride the Riccardi brings home to-day."

Hair in heaps lay heavily
Over a pale brow spirit-pure—
Carved like the heart of the coal-black tree,

Crisped like a war-steed's encolure—
And vainly sought to dissemble her eyes
Of the blackest black our eyes endure.

And lo, a blade for a knight's emprise
Filled the fine empty sheath of a man,—
The Duke grew straightway brave and wise.

He looked at her, as a lover can ;
She looked at him, as one who awakes :
The past was a sleep, and her life began.

Now, love so ordered for both their sakes,
A feast was held that selfsame night
In the pile which the mighty shadow makes.

(For Via Larga is three-parts light,
But the palace overshadows one,
Because of a crime which may God requite !

To Florence and God the wrong was done,
Through the first republic's murder there
By Cosimo and his cursed son.)

The Duke (with the statue's face in the square)
Turned in the midst of his multitude
At the bright approach of the bridal pair.

Face to face the lovers stood
A single minute and no more,
While the bridegroom bent as a man subdued—

Bowed till his bonnet brushed the floor—
For the Duke on the lady a kiss conferred,
As the courtly custom was of yore.

In a minute can lovers exchange a word ?
If a word did pass, which I do not think,
Only one out of the thousand heard.

That was the bridegroom.   At day's brink
He and his bride were alone at last
In a bed-chamber by a taper's blink.

Calmly he said that her lot was cast,
That the door she had passed was shut on her
Till the final catafalk repassed.

The world meanwhile, its noise and stir,
Through a certain window facing the East
She could watch like a convent's chronicler.

Since passing the door might lead to a feast,
And a feast might lead to so much beside,
He, of many evils, chose the least.

" Freely I choose too," said the bride—
" Your window and its world suffice,"
Replied the tongue, while the heart replied—

" If I spend the night with that devil twice,
May his window serve as my loop of hell
Whence a damned soul looks on paradise !

" I fly to the Duke who loves me well,
Sit by his side and laugh at sorrow
Ere I count another ave-bell.

" 'Tis only the coat of a page to borrow,
And tie my hair in a horse-boy's trim,
And I save my soul—but not to-morrow "—

(She checked herself and her eye grew dim)
" My father tarries to bless my state :
I must keep it one day more for him.

" Is one day more so long to wait ?
Moreover the Duke rides past, I know ;
We shall see each other, sure as fate."

She turned on her side and slept.   Just so !
So we resolve on a thing and sleep :
So did the lady, ages ago.

That night the Duke said, " Dear or cheap
As the cost of this cup of bliss may prove
To body or soul, I will drain it deep."

And on the morrow, bold with love,
He beckoned the bridegroom (close on call,
As his duty bade, by the Duke's alcove)

And smiled " 'Twas a very funeral,
Your lady will think, this feast of ours,—
A shame to efface, whate'er befall !

" What if we break from the Arno bowers,
And try if Petraja, cool and green,
Cure last night's fault with this morning's flowers ? "

The bridegroom, not a thought to be seen
On his steady brow and quiet mouth,
Said, " Too much favour for me so mean !

" But, alas ! my lady leaves the South ;
Each wind that comes from the Apennine
Is a menace to her tender youth :

" Nor a way exists, the wise opine,
If she quits her palace twice this year,
To avert the flower of life's decline."

Quoth the Duke, " A sage and a kindly fear.
Moreover Petraja is cold this spring :
Be our feast to-night as usual here ! "

And then to himself—" Which night shall bring
Thy bride to her lover's embraces, fool—
Or I am the fool, and thou art the king !

" Yet my passion must wait a night, nor cool—
For to-night the Envoy arrives from France,
Whose heart I unlock with thyself, my tool.

" I need thee still and might miss perchance.
To-day is not wholly lost, beside,
With its hope of my lady's countenance :

" For I ride—what should I do but ride ?
And passing her palace, if I list,
May glance at its window—well betide ! "

So said, so done ; nor the lady missed
One ray that broke from the ardent brow,
Nor a curl of the lips where the spirit kissed.

Be sure that each renewed the vow,
No morrow's sun should arise and set
And leave them then as it left them now.

But next day passed, and next day yet,
With still fresh cause to wait one day more
Ere each leaped over the parapet.

And still, as love's brief morning wore,
With a gentle start, half smile, half sigh,
They found love not as it seemed before.

They thought it would work infallibly,
But not in despite of heaven and earth :
The rose would blow when the storm passed by.

Meantime they could profit in winter's dearth
By store of fruits that supplant the rose :
The world and its ways have a certain worth :

And to press a point while these oppose
Were simple policy ; better wait :
We lose no friends and we gain no foes.

Meantime, worse fates than a lover's fate,
Who daily may ride and pass and look
Where his lady watches behind the grate !

And she—she watched the square like a book,
Holding one picture and only one,
Which daily to find she undertook :

When the picture was reached the book was done,
And she turned from the picture at night to scheme
Of tearing it out for herself next sun.

So weeks grew months, years ; gleam by gleam
The glory dropped from their youth and love,
And both perceived they had dreamed a dream ;

Which hovered as dreams do, still above :
But who can take a dream for a truth ?
Oh, hide our eyes from the next remove !

One day as the lady saw her youth
Depart, and the silver thread that streaked
Her hair, and, worn by the serpent's tooth,

The brow so puckered, the chin so peaked,—
And wondered who the woman was,
Hollow-eyed and haggard-cheeked,

Fronting her silent in the glass—
" Summon here," she suddenly said,
" Before the rest of my old self pass,

" Him, the Carver, a hand to aid,
Who fashions the clay no love will change,
And fixes a beauty never to fade.

" Let Robbia's craft so apt and strange
Arrest the remains of young and fair,
And rivet them while the seasons range.

" Make me a face on the window there,
Waiting as ever, mute the while,
My love to pass below in the square !

" And let me think that it may beguile
Dreary days which the dead must spend
Down in their darkness under the aisle,

" To say, ' What matters it at the end ?
I did no more while my heart was warm
Than does that image, my pale-faced friend.'

" Where is the use of the lip's red charm,
The heaven of hair, the pride of the brow,
And the blood that blues the inside arm—

" Unless we turn, as the soul knows how,
The earthly gift to an end divine ?
A lady of clay is as good, I trow."

But long ere Robbia's cornice, fine
With flowers and fruits which leaves enlace,
Was set where now is the empty shrine—

(And, leaning out of a bright blue space,
As a ghost might lean from a chink of sky,
The passionate pale lady's face—

Eyeing ever, with earnest eye
And quick-turned neck at its breathless stretch,
Some one who ever is passing by—)

The Duke had sighed like the simplest wretch
In Florence, " Youth—my dream escapes !
Will its record stay ? "   And he bade them fetch

Some subtle moulder of brazen shapes—
" Can the soul, the will, die out of a man
Ere his body find the grave that gapes ?

" John of Douay shall effect my plan,
Set me on horseback here aloft,
Alive, as the crafty sculptor can,

" In the very square I have crossed so oft :
That men may admire, when future suns
Shall touch the eyes to a purpose soft,

" While the mouth and the brow stay brave in
    bronze—
Admire and say, ' When he was alive
How he would take his pleasure once ! '

" And it shall go hard but I contrive
To listen the while, and laugh in my tomb
At idleness which aspires to strive."

So ! While these wait the trump of doom,
How do their spirits pass, I wonder,
Nights and days in the narrow room ?

Still, I suppose, they sit and ponder
What a gift life was, ages ago,
Six steps out of the chapel yonder.

Only they see not God, I know,
Nor all that chivalry of his,
The soldier-saints who, row on row,

Burn upward each to his point of bliss—
Since, the end of life being manifest,
He had burned his way thro' the world to this.

I hear you reproach, " But delay was best,
For their end was a crime."—Oh, a crime will do
As well, I reply, to serve for a test,

As a virtue golden through and through,
Sufficient to vindicate itself
And prove its worth at a moment's view !

Must a game be played for the sake of pelf ?
Where a button goes, 'twere an epigram
To offer the stamp of the very Guelph.

The true has no value beyond the sham :
As well the counter as coin, I submit,
When your table's a hat, and your prize, a dram.

Stake your counter as boldly every whit,
Venture as warily, use the same skill,
Do your best, whether winning or losing it,

If you choose to play !—is my principle.
Let a man contend to the uttermost
For his life's set prize, be it what it will !

The counter our lovers staked was lost
As surely as if it were lawful coin ;
And the sin I impute to each frustrate ghost

Is, the unlit lamp and the ungirt loin,
Though the end in sight was a vice, I say.
You of the virtue (we issue join)
How strive you ?   *De te, fabula !*

ROBERT BROWNING.

LOVE AND DUTY

OF love that never found his earthly close,
What sequel ?   Streaming eyes and breaking hearts ?
Or all the same as if he had not been ?
    Not so.   Shall Error in the round of time
Still father Truth ?   Oh shall the braggart shout
For some blind glimpse of freedom work itself
Through madness, hated by the wise, to law
System and empire ?   Sin itself be found
The cloudy porch oft opening on the Sun ?
And only he, this wonder, dead, become
Mere highway dust ? or year by year alone

Sit brooding in the ruins of a life,
Nightmare of youth, the spectre of himself ?
  If this were thus, if this, indeed, were all,
Better the narrow brain, the stony heart,
The staring eye glazed o'er with sapless days,
The long mechanic pacings to and fro,
The set grey life, and apathetic end.
But am I not the nobler through thy love ?
Oh three times less unworthy ! likewise thou
Art more through Love, and greater than thy years.
The Sun will run his orbit, and the Moon
Her circle. Wait, and Love himself will bring
The drooping flower of knowledge changed to fruit
Of wisdom. Wait : my faith is large in Time,
And that which shapes it to some perfect end.
  Will some one say, then why not ill for good ?
Why took ye not your pastime ? To that man
My work shall answer, since I knew the right
And did it ; for a man is not as God,
But then most Godlike being most a man.
—So let me think 'tis well for thee and me—
Ill-fated that I am, what lot is mine
Whose foresight preaches peace, my heart so slow
To feel it ! For how hard it seem'd to me,
When eyes, love-languid through half-tears, would
    dwell
One earnest, earnest moment upon mine,
Then not to dare to see ! when thy low voice,
Faltering, would break its syllables, to keep
My own full-tuned,—hold passion in a leash,
And not leap forth and fall about thy neck,
And on thy bosom (deep-desired relief !)
Rain out the heavy mist of tears, that weigh'd
Upon my brain, my senses, and my soul !
  For Love himself took part against himself
To warn us off, and Duty loved of Love—
Oh this world's curse,—beloved but hated—came
Like Death betwixt thy dear embrace and mine,

And crying, " Who is this ? behold thy bride,"
She push'd me from thee.

                              If the sense is hard
To alien ears, I did not speak to these—
No, not to thee, but to thyself in me :
Hard is my doom and thine : thou knowest it all.
    Could Love part thus ? was it not well to speak,
To have spoken once ? It could not but be well.
The slow sweet hours that bring us all things good,
The slow sad hours that bring us all things ill,
And all good things from evil, brought the night
In which we sat together and alone,
And to the want, that hollow'd all the heart,
Gave utterance by the yearning of an eye,
That burn'd upon its object through such tears
As flow but once a life.

                              The trance gave way
To those caresses, when a hundred times
In that last kiss, which never was the last,
Farewell, like endless welcome, lived and died.
Then follow'd counsel, comfort, and the words
That make a man feel strong in speaking truth ;
Till now the dark was worn, and overhead
The lights of sunset and of sunrise mix'd
In that brief night ; the summer night, that paused
Among her stars to hear us ; stars that hung
Love-charm'd to listen : all the wheels of Time
Spun round in station, but the end had come.
    Oh then like those, who clench their nerves to rush
Upon their dissolution, we two rose,
There—closing like an individual life—
In one blind cry of passion and of pain,
Like bitter accusation ev'n to death,
Caught up the whole of love and utter'd it,
And bade adieu for ever !

                              Live—yet live
Shall sharpest pathos blight us, knowing all
Life needs for life is possible to will—

Live happy ; tend thy flowers ; be tended by
My blessing ! Should my Shadow cross thy thoughts
Too sadly for their peace, remand it thou
For calmer hours to Memory's darkest hold,
If not to be forgotten—not at once—
Not all forgotten. Should it cross thy dreams,
Oh might it come like one that looks content,
With quiet eyes unfaithful to the truth,
And point thee forward to a distant light,
Or seem to lift a burthen from thy heart
And leave thee freër, till thou wake refresh'd,
Then when the first low matin-chirp hath grown
Full quire, and morning driv'n her plow of pearl
Far furrowing into light the mounded rack,
Beyond the fair green field and eastern sea.

LORD TENNYSON.

LOVE AMONG THE RUINS

WHERE the quiet-coloured end of evening smiles
  Miles and miles
On the solitary pastures where our sheep
  Half-asleep
Tinkle homeward thro' the twilight, stray or stop
  As they crop—
Was the site once of a city great and gay,
  (So they say)
Of our country's very capital, its prince
  Ages since
Held his court in, gathered councils, wielding far
  Peace or war.

Now—the country does not even boast a tree,
  As you see,
To distinguish slopes of verdure, certain rills
  From the hills

Intersect and give a name to, (else they run
        Into one)
Where the domed and daring palace shot its spires
        Up like fires
O'er the hundred-gated circuit of a wall
        Bounding all,
Made of marble, men might march on nor be pressed,
        Twelve abreast.

And such plenty and perfection, see, of grass
        Never was !
Such a carpet as, this summer-time, o'erspreads
        And embeds
Every vestige of the city, guessed alone,
        Stock or stone—
Where a multitude of men breathed joy and woe
        Long ago ;
Lust of glory pricked their hearts up, dread of shame
        Struck them tame ;
And that glory and that shame alike, the gold
        Bought and sold.

Now,—the single little turret that remains
        On the plains,
By the caper overrooted, by the gourd
        Overscored,
While the patching houseleek's head of blossom winks
        Through the chinks—
Marks the basement whence a tower in ancient time
        Sprang sublime,
And a burning ring, all round, the chariots traced
        As they raced,
And the monarch and his minions and his dames
        Viewed the games.

And I know, while thus the quiet-coloured eve
        Smiles to leave

To their folding, all our many tinkling fleece
    In such peace,
And the slopes and rills in undistinguished grey
    Melt away—
That a girl with eager eyes and yellow hair
    Waits me there
In the turret whence the charioteers caught soul
    For the goal,
When the king looked, where she looks now, breath-
       less, dumb
    Till I come.

But he looked upon the city, every side,
    Far and wide,
All the mountains topped with temples, all the glades'
    Colonnades,
All the causeys, bridges, aqueducts,—and then,
    All the men !
When I do come, she will speak not, she will stand,
    Either hand
On my shoulder, give her eyes the first embrace
    Of my face,
Ere we rush, ere we extinguish sight and speech
    Each on each.

In one year they sent a million fighters forth
    South and North,
And they built their gods a brazen pillar high
    As the sky,
Yet reserved a thousand chariots in full force—
    Gold, of course.
Oh heart ! oh blood that freezes, blood that burns !
    Earth's returns
For whole centuries of folly, noise and sin !
    Shut them in,
With their triumphs and their glories and the rest !
    Love is best.

               ROBERT BROWNING.

THE LAST RIDE TOGETHER

I SAID—Then, dearest, since 'tis so,
Since now at length my fate I know,
Since nothing all my love avails,
Since all, my life seemed meant for, fails,
  Since this was written and needs must be—
My whole heart rises up to bless
Your name in pride and thankfulness !
Take back the hope you gave,—I claim
Only a memory of the same,
—And this beside, if you will not blame,
  Your leave for one more last ride with me.

My mistress bent that brow of hers ;
Those deep dark eyes where pride demurs
When pity would be softening through,
Fixed me a breathing-while or two
  With life or death in the balance : right !
The blood replenished me again ;
My last thought was at least not vain :
I and my mistress, side by side
Shall be together, breathe and ride,
So, one day more am I deified.
  Who knows but the world may end to-night ?

Hush ! if you saw some western cloud
All billowy-bosomed, over-bowed
By many benedictions—sun's
And moon's and evening-star's at once—
  And so, you, looking and loving best,
Conscious grew, your passion drew
Cloud, sunset, moonrise, star-shine too,
Down on you, near and yet more near,
Till flesh must fade for heaven was here !—

Thus leant she and lingered—joy and fear !
    Thus lay she a moment on my breast.

Then we began to ride. My soul
Smoothed itself out, a long-cramped scroll
Freshening and fluttering in the wind.
Past hopes already lay behind.
    What need to strive with a life awry ?
Had I said that, had I done this,
So might I gain, so might I miss.
Might she have loved me ? just as well
She might have hated, who can tell !
Where had I been now if the worst befell ?
    And here we are riding, she and I.

Fail I alone, in words and deeds ?
Why, all men strive and who succeeds ?
We rode ; it seemed my spirit flew,
Saw other regions, cities new,
    As the world rushed by on either side.
I thought,—All labour, yet no less
Bear up beneath their unsuccess.
Look at the end of work, contrast
The petty done, the undone vast,
This present of theirs with the hopeful past !
    I hoped she would love me ; here we ride.

What hand and brain went ever paired ?
What heart alike conceived and dared ?
What act proved all its thought had been ?
What will but felt the fleshly screen ?
    We ride and I see her bosom heave.
There's many a crown for who can reach.
Ten lines, a statesman's life in each !
The flag stuck on a heap of bones,
A soldier's doing ! what atones ?
They scratch his name on the Abbey-stones.
    My riding is better, by their leave.

What does it all mean, poet ?   Well,
Your brains beat into rhythm, you tell
What we felt only ; you expressed
You hold things beautiful the best,
    And pace them in rhyme so, side by side.
'Tis something, nay 'tis much : but then,
Have you yourself what's best for men ?
Are you—poor, sick, old ere your time—
Nearer one whit your own sublime
Than we who never have turned a rhyme ?
    Sing, riding's a joy ! For me, I ride.

And you, great sculptor,—so, you gave
A score of years to Art, her slave,
And that's your Venus, whence we turn
To yonder girl that fords the burn !
    You acquiesce, and shall I repine ?
What, man of music, you grown grey
With notes and nothing else to say,
Is this your sole praise from a friend,
" Greatly his opera's strains intend,
But in music we know how fashions end ! "
    I gave my youth ; but we ride, in fine.

Who knows what's fit for us ?   Had fate
Proposed bliss here should sublimate
My being—had I signed the bond—
Still one must lead some life beyond,
    Have a bliss to die with, dim-descried.
This foot once planted on the goal,
This glory-garland round my soul,
Could I descry such ? Try and test !
I sink back shuddering from the quest.
Earth being so good, would heaven seem best ?
    Now, heaven and she are beyond this ride.

And yet—she has not spoke so long !
What if heaven be that, fair and strong

At life's best, with our eyes upturned
Whither life's flower is first discerned,
   We, fixed so, ever should so abide ?
What if we still ride on, we two,
With life for ever old yet new,
Changed not in kind but in degree,
The instant made eternity,—
And heaven just prove that I and she
   Ride, ride together, for ever ride ?

ROBERT BROWNING.

ELAINE

(From " The Idylls of the King ")

[Elaine, who has fallen in love with Lancelot, goes to tend him after he has been wounded in battle.]

THEN rose Elaine and glided through the fields,
And pass'd beneath the wildly-sculptured gates
Far up the dim rich city to her kin ;
There bode the night : but woke with dawn, and pass'd
Down through the dim rich city to the fields,
Thence to the cave : so day by day she pass'd
In either twilight ghost-like to and fro
Gliding, and every day she tended him,
And likewise many a night : and Lancelot
Would, though he call'd his wound a little hurt
Whereof he should be quickly whole, at times
Brain-feverous in his heat and agony, seem
Uncourteous, even he : but the meek maid
Sweetly forbore him ever, being to him
Meeker than any child to a rough nurse,
Milder than any mother to a sick child,
And never woman yet, since man's first fall,
Did kindlier unto man, but her deep love

Upbore her ; till the hermit, skill'd in all
The simples and the science of that time,
Told him that her fine care had saved his life.
And the sick man forgot her simple blush,
Would call her friend and sister, sweet Elaine,
Would listen for her coming, and regret
Her parting step, and held her tenderly,
And loved her with all love except the love
Of man and woman when they love their best,
Closest and sweetest, and had died the death
In any knightly fashion for her sake.
And peradventure had he seen her first,
She might have made this and that other world
Another world for the sick man ; but now
The shackles of an old love straiten'd him,
His honour rooted in dishonour stood,
And faith unfaithful kept him falsely true.

  Yet the great knight in his mid-sickness made
Full many a holy vow and pure resolve.
These, as but born of sickness, could not live :
For when the blood ran lustier in him again,
Full often the sweet image of one face,
Making a treacherous quiet in his heart,
Dispersed his resolution like a cloud.
Then if the maiden, while that ghostly grace
Beam'd on his fancy, spoke, he answer'd not,
Or short and coldly, and she knew right well
What the rough sickness meant, but what this meant
She knew not, and the sorrow dimm'd her sight,
And drave her ere her time across the fields
Far into the rich city, where alone
She murmur'd, " Vain, in vain : it cannot be.
He will not love me : how then ? must I die ? "
Then as a little helpless innocent bird,
That has but one plain passage of few notes,
Will sing the simple passage o'er and o'er
For all an April morning, till the ear

Wearies to hear it, so the simple maid
Went half the night repeating, " Must I die ? "
And now to right she turn'd, and now to left,
And found no ease in turning or in rest ;
And " Him or death," she mutter'd, " death or him,"
Again and like a burden, " Him or death."

But when Sir Lancelot's deadly hurt was whole,
To Astolat returning rode the three.
There morn by morn, arraying her sweet self
In that wherein she deem'd she look'd her best,
She came before Sir Lancelot, for she thought,
" If I be loved, these are my festal robes ;
If not, the victim's flowers before he fall."
And Lancelot ever press'd upon the maid
That she should ask some goodly gift of him
For her own self or hers ; " and do not shun
To speak the wish most near to your true heart ;
Such service have you done me, that I make
My will of yours, and Prince and Lord am I
In mine own land, and what I will I can."
Then like a ghost she lifted up her face,
But like a ghost without the power to speak.
And Lancelot saw that she withheld her wish,
And bode among them yet a little space
Till he should learn it ; and one morn it chanced
He found her in among the garden yews,
And said, " Delay no longer, speak your wish,
Seeing I must go to-day : " then out she brake :
" Going ? and we shall never see you more.
And I must die for want of one bold word."
" Speak : that I live to hear," he said, " is yours."
Then suddenly and passionately she spoke :
" I have gone mad. I love you : let me die."
" Ah, sister," answer'd Lancelot, " what is this ? "
And innocently extending her white arms,
" Your love," she said, " your love—to be your wife."
And Lancelot answer'd, " Had I chosen to wed,

I had been wedded earlier, sweet Elaine :
But now there never will be wife of mine."
" No, no," she cried, " I care not to be wife,
But to be with you still, to see your face,
To serve you, and to follow you through the world."
And Lancelot answer'd, " Nay, the world, the world,
All ear and eye, with such a stupid heart
To interpret ear and eye, and such a tongue
To blare its own interpretation—nay,
Full ill then should I quit your brother's love,
And your good father's kindness." And she said,
" Not to be with you, not to see your face—
Alas for me then, my good days are done."
" Nay, noble maid," he answer'd, " ten times nay !
This is not love : but love's first flash in youth,
Most common : yea, I know it of mine own self :
And you yourself will smile at your own self
Hereafter, when you yield your flower of life
To one more fitly yours, not thrice your age :
And then will I, for true you are and sweet
Beyond mine old belief in womanhood,
More specially should your good knight be poor,
Endow you with broad land and territory
Even to the half my realm beyond the seas,
So that would make you happy : furthermore,
Ev'n to the death, as though you were my blood,
In all your quarrels will I be your knight.
This will I do, dear damsel, for your sake,
And more than this I cannot."

                    While he spoke
She neither blush'd nor shook, but deathly pale
Stood grasping what was nearest, then replied :
" Of all this will I nothing ; " and so fell,
And thus they bore her swooning to her tower.

Then spake, to whom through those black walls of
    yew
Their talk had pierced, her father : " Ay, a flash,

I fear me, that will strike my blossom dead.
Too courteous are you, fair Lord Lancelot.
I pray you, use some rough discourtesy
To blunt or break her passion."

       Lancelot said,
" That were against me : what I can I will ; "
And there that day remain'd, and toward even
Sent for his shield : full meekly rose the maid,
Stripp'd off the case, and gave the naked shield ;
Then, when she heard his horse upon the stones,
Unclasping flung the casement back, and look'd
Down on his helm, from which her sleeve had gone.
And Lancelot knew the little clinking sound ;
And she by tact of love was well aware
That Lancelot knew that she was looking at him.
And yet he glanced not up, nor waved his hand,
Nor bade farewell, but sadly rode away.
This was the one discourtesy that he used.

So in her tower alone the maiden sat :
His very shield was gone ; only the case,
Her own poor work, her empty labour, left.
But still she heard him, still his picture form'd
And grew between her and the pictured wall.
Then came her father, saying in low tones,
" Have comfort," whom she greeted quietly.
Then came her brethren saying, " Peace to thee,
Sweet sister," whom she answer'd with all calm.
But when they left her to herself again,
Death, like a friend's voice from a distant field
Approaching through the darkness, call'd ; the owls
Wailing had power upon her, and she mix'd
Her fancies with the sallow-rifted glooms
Of evening, and the moanings of the wind.

And in those days she made a little song,
And call'd her song " The Song of Love and Death,"
And sang it : sweetly could she make and sing.

" Sweet is true love though given in vain, in vain ;
And sweet is death who puts an end to pain :
I know not which is sweeter, no, not I.

" Love, art thou sweet ? then bitter death must be :
Love, thou art bitter ; sweet is death to me.
O Love, if death be sweeter, let me die.

" Sweet love, that seems not made to fade away,
Sweet death, that seems to make us loveless clay,
I know not which is sweeter, no, not I.

" I fain would follow love, if that could be ;
I needs must follow death, who calls for me ;
Call and I follow, I follow ! let me die."

High with the last line scaled her voice, and this,
All in a fiery dawning wild with wind
That shook her tower, the brothers heard, and thought
With shuddering, " Hark the Phantom of the house
That ever shrieks before a death," and call'd
The father, and all three in hurry and fear
Ran to her, and lo ! the blood-red light of dawn
Flared on her face, she shrilling, " Let me die ! "

As when we dwell upon a word we know,
Repeating, till the word we know so well
Becomes a wonder, and we know not why,
So dwelt the father on her face, and thought,
" Is this Elaine ? " till back the maiden fell,
Then gave a languid hand to each, and lay,
Speaking a still good-morrow with her eyes.
At last she said, " Sweet brothers, yesternight
I seem'd a curious little maid again,
As happy as when we dwelt among the woods,
And when you used to take me with the flood
Up the great river in the boatman's boat.
Only you would not pass beyond the cape

That has the poplar on it : there you fix'd
Your limit, oft returning with the tide.
And yet I cried because you would not pass
Beyond it, and far up the shining flood
Until we found the palace of the King.
And yet you would not ; but this night I dream'd
That I was all alone upon the flood,
And then I said, ' Now shall I have my will : '
And there I woke, but still the wish remain'd.
So let me hence, that I may pass at last
Beyond the poplar and far up the flood,
Until I find the palace of the King.
There will I enter in among them all,
And no man there will dare to mock at me ;
But there the fine Gawain will wonder at me,
And there the great Sir Lancelot muse at me—
Gawain, who bade a thousand farewells to me ;
Lancelot, who coldly went, nor bade me one :
And there the King will know me and my love,
And there the Queen herself will pity me,
And all the gentle court will welcome me,
And after my long voyage I shall rest ! "

" Peace," said her father, " O my child, you seem
Light-headed, for what force is yours to go
So far, being sick ? and wherefore would you look
On this proud fellow again, who scorns us all ? "

Then the rough Torre began to heave and move,
And bluster into stormy sobs and say,
" I never loved him : an I mete with him,
I care not however great he be,
Then will I strike at him and strike him down,
Give me good fortune, I will strike him dead,
For this discomfort he hath done the house."

To which the gentle sister made reply,
" Fret not yourself, dear brother, nor be wroth,

Seeing it is no more Sir Lancelot's fault
Not to love me, than it is mine to love
Him of all men who seems to me the highest."

" Highest?" the father answer'd, echoing, "highest?"
(He meant to break the passion in her) ; " nay,
Daughter, I know not what you call the highest ;
But this I know, for all the people know it,
He loves the Queen, and in an open shame :
And she returns his love in open shame ;
If this be high, what is it to be low ? "

Then spake the lily maid of Astolat :
" Sweet father, all too faint and sick am I
For anger : these are slanders : never yet
Was noble man but made ignoble talk.
He makes no friend who never made a foe.
But now it is my glory to have loved
One peerless, without stain : so let me pass,
My father, howsoe'er I seem to you,
Not all unhappy, having loved God's best
And greatest, though my love had no return :
Yet, seeing you desire your child to live,
Thanks, but you work against your own desire ;
For if I could believe the things you say,
I should but die the sooner ; wherefore cease,
Sweet father, and bid call the ghostly man
Hither, and let me shrive me clean, and die."

So when the ghostly man had come and gone,
She with a face, bright as for sin forgiven,
Besought Lavaine to write as she devised
A letter, word for word ; and when he ask'd,
" Is it for Lancelot, is it for my dear lord ?
Then will I bear it gladly," she replied,
" For Lancelot and the Queen and all the world,
But I myself must bear it." Then he wrote

The letter she devised ; which being writ
And folded, " O sweet father, tender and true,
Deny me not," she said—" you never yet
Denied my fancies—this, however strange,
My latest : lay the letter in my hand
A little ere I die, and close the hand
Upon it ; I shall guard it even in death.
And when the heat is gone from out my heart,
Then take the little bed on which I died
For Lancelot's love, and deck it like the Queen's
For richness, and me also like the Queen
In all I have of rich, and lay me on it.
And let there be prepared a chariot-bier
To take me to the river, and a barge
Be ready on the river, clothed in black.
I go in state to court, to meet the Queen.
There surely I shall speak for mine own self,
And none of you can speak for me so well.
And therefore let our dumb old man alone
Go with me, he can steer and row, and he
Will guide me to that palace, to the doors."

She ceased : her father promised ; whereupon
She grew so cheerful that they deem'd her death
Was rather in the fantasy than the blood.
But ten slow mornings pass'd, and on the eleventh
Her father laid the letter in her hand,
And closed the hand upon it, and she died.
So that day there was dole in Astolat.

But when the next sun brake from underground,
Then, those two brethren slowly with bent brows
Accompanying, the sad chariot-bier
Pass'd like a shadow through the field, that shone
Full-summer, to that stream whereon the barge,
Pall'd all its length in blackest samite, lay.
There sat the lifelong creature of the house,

Loyal, the dumb old servitor on deck,
Winking his eyes, and twisted all his face.
So those two brethren from the chariot took
And on the black decks laid her in her bed,
Set in her hand a lily, o'er her hung
The silken case with braided blazonings,
And kiss'd her quiet brows, and saying to her,
" Sister, farewell for ever," and again
" Farewell, sweet sister," parted all in tears.
Then rose the dumb old servitor, and the dead,
Steer'd by the dumb, went upward with the flood—
In her right hand the lily, in her left
The letter—all her bright hair streaming down—
And all the coverlid was cloth of gold
Drawn to her waist, and she herself in white
All but her face, and that clear-featured face
Was lovely, for she did not seem as dead,
But fast asleep, and lay as though she smiled.

Lord Tennyson.

POMPILIA

(*From " The Ring and the Book "*)

[Pompilia, at the age of twelve, has been married by
her parents to Count Guido Franceschini. The parents
are attracted by the aristocratic connection, the Count
expects financial benefits. Being baulked of the money,
Guido vents his wrath on Pompilia, who, in desperation,
seeks the assistance of a priest, Caponsacchi, to enable
her to fly to Rome. Guido gives chase and overtakes
them. In the end he fatally wounds Pompilia and kills
her parents. Pompilia, dying in hospital, has been telling
the story of her life.]

Well, and there is more ! Yes, my end of breath
Shall bear away my soul in being true !
He is still here, not outside with the world,

Here, here, I have him in his rightful place !
'Tis now, when I am most upon the move,
I feel for what I verily find—again
The face, again the eyes, again, through all,
The heart and its immeasurable love
Of my one friend, my only, all my own,
Who put his breast between the spears and me.
Ever with Caponsacchi ! Otherwise
Here alone would be failure, loss to me—
How much more loss to him, with life debarred
From giving life, love locked from love's display,
The day-star stopped its task that makes night morn !
O lover of my life, O soldier-saint,
No work begun shall ever pause for death !
Love will be helpful to me more and more
I' the coming course, the new path I must tread,
My weak hand in thy strong hand, strong for that !
Tell him that if I seem without him now,
That's the world's insight ! Oh, he understands !
He is at Civita—do I once doubt
The world again is holding us apart ?
He had been here, displayed in my behalf
The broad brow that reverberates the truth,
And flashed the word God gave him, back to man !
I know where the free soul is flown ! My fate
Will have been hard for even him to bear :
Let it confirm him in the trust of God,
Showing how holily he dared the deed !
And, for the rest,—say, from the deed, no touch
Of harm came, but all good, all happiness,
Not one faint fleck of failure ! Why explain ?
What I see, oh, he sees and how much more !
Tell him,—I know not wherefore the true word
Should fade and fall unuttered at the last—
It was the name of him I sprang to meet
When came the knock, the summons and the end.
" My great heart, my strong hand are back again ! "
I would have sprung to these, beckoning across

Murder and hell gigantic and distinct
O' the threshold, posted to exclude me heaven :
He is ordained to call and I to come !
Do not the dead wear flowers when dressed for God ?
Say,—I am all in flowers from head to foot !
Say,—not one flower of all he said and did,
Might seem to flit unnoticed, fade unknown,
But dropped a seed has grown a balsam-tree
Whereof the blossoming perfumes the place
At this supreme of moments ! He is a priest ;
He cannot marry therefore, which is right :
I think he would not marry if he could.
Marriage on earth seems such a counterfeit,
Mere imitation of the inimitable :
In heaven we have the real and true and sure.
'Tis there they neither marry nor are given
In marriage but are as the angels : right,
Oh how right that is, how like Jesus Christ
To say that ! Marriage-making for the earth,
With gold so much,—birth, power, repute so much,
Or beauty, youth so much, in lack of these !
Be as the angels rather, who, apart,
Know themselves into one, are found at length
Married, but marry never, no, nor give
In marriage ; they are man and wife at once
When the true time is : here we have to wait
Not so long neither ! Could we by a wish
Have what we will and get the future now,
Would we wish aught done undone in the past ?
So, let him wait God's instant men call years ;
Meantime hold hard by truth and his great soul,
Do out the duty ! Through such souls alone
God stooping shows sufficient of His light
For us i' the dark to rise by. And I rise.

                              ROBERT BROWNING.

GUINEVERE

(*From " The Idylls of the King "*)

[Queen Guinevere, having sinned with Lancelot, the disloyal knight, flies to a convent at Almesbury. King Arthur, her husband, follows and finds her there.]

SHE made her face a darkness from the King :
And in the darkness heard his armed feet
Pause by her ; then came silence, then a voice,
Monotonous and hollow like a Ghost's
Denouncing judgment, but though changed, the
  King's :

" Liest thou here so low, the child of one
I honour'd, happy, dead before thy shame ?
Well is it that no child is born of thee.
The children born of thee are sword and fire,
Red ruin, and the breaking up of laws,
The craft of kindred and the Godless hosts
Of heathen swarming o'er the Northern Sea ;
Whom I, while yet Sir Lancelot, my right arm,
The mightiest of my knights, abode with me,
Have everywhere about this land of Christ
In twelve great battles ruining overthrown.
And knowest thou now from whence I come—from
  him,
From waging bitter war with him ; and he,
That did not shun to smite me in worse way,
Had yet that grace of courtesy in him left,
He spared to lift his hand against the King
Who made him knight : but many a knight was slain ;
And many more, and all his kith and kin
Clave to him, and abode in his own land.
And many more when Modred raised revolt,

Forgetful of their troth and fealty, clave
To Modred, and a remnant stays with me.
And of this remnant will I leave a part,
True men who love me still, for whom I live,
To guard thee in the wild hour coming on,
Lest but a hair of this low head be harm'd.
Fear not ; thou shalt be guarded till my death.
Howbeit I know, if ancient prophecies
Have err'd not, that I march to meet my doom.
Thou hast not made my life so sweet to me,
That I the King should greatly care to live ;
For thou hast spoilt the purpose of my life.
Bear with me for the last time while I show,
Ev'n for thy sake, the sin which thou hast sinn'd.
For when the Roman left us, and their law
Relax'd its hold upon us, and the ways
Were fill'd with rapine, here and there a deed
Of prowess done redress'd a random wrong.
But I was first of all the kings who drew
The knighthood-errant of this realm and all
The realms together under me, their Head,
In that fair Order of my Table Round,
A glorious company, the flower of men,
To serve as model for the mighty world,
And be the fair beginning of a time.
I made them lay their hands in mine and swear
To reverence the King, as if he were
Their conscience, and their conscience as their King,
To break the heathen and uphold the Christ,
To ride abroad redressing human wrongs,
To speak no slander, no, nor listen to it,
To lead sweet lives in purest chastity,
To love one maiden only, cleave to her,
And worship her by years of noble deeds,
Until they won her ; for indeed I knew
Of no more subtle master under heaven
Than is the maiden passion for a maid,
Not only to keep down the base in man,

But teach high thought, and amiable words
And courtliness, and the desire of fame,
And love of truth, and all that makes a man.
And all this throve until I wedded thee,
Believing, ' lo mine helpmate, one to feel
My purpose and rejoicing in my joy.'
Then came thy shameful sin with Lancelot ;
Then came the sin of Tristram and Isolt ;
Then others, following these my mightiest knights,
And drawing foul ensample from fair names,
Sinn'd also, till the loathsome opposite
Of all my heart had destined did obtain,
And all through thee ! so that this life of mine
I guard as God's high gift from scathe and wrong,
Not greatly care to lose ; but rather think
How sad it were for Arthur, should he live,
To sit once more within his lonely hall,
And miss the wonted number of my knights,
And miss to hear high talk of noble deeds
As in the golden days before thy sin.
For which of us, who might be left, could speak
Of the pure heart, nor seem to glance at thee ?
And in thy bowers of Camelot or of Usk
Thy shadow still would glide from room to room,
And I should evermore be vex'd with thee
In hanging robe or vacant ornament,
Or ghostly footfall echoing on the stair.
For think not, though thou wouldst not love thy lord,
Thy lord has wholly lost his love for thee.
I am not made of so slight elements.
Yet must I leave thee, woman, to thy shame.
I hold that man the worst of public foes
Who either for his own or children's sake,
To save his blood from scandal, lets the wife
Whom he knows false abide and rule the house :
For being through his cowardice allow'd
Her station, taken everywhere for pure,
She like a new disease, unknown to men,

Creeps, no precaution used, among the crowd,
Makes wicked lightnings of her eyes, and saps
The fealty of our friends, and stirs the pulse
With devil's leaps, and poisons half the young.
Worst of the worst were that man he that reigns !
Better the King's waste hearth and aching heart
Than thou reseated in thy place of light,
The mockery of my people, and their bane."

He paused, and in the pause she crept an inch
Nearer, and laid her hands about his feet.
Far off a solitary trumpet blew.
Then waiting by the doors the war-horse neigh'd
As at a friend's voice, and he spake again :

" Yet think not that I come to urge thy crimes,
I did not come to curse thee, Guinevere,
I, whose vast pity almost makes me die
To see thee, laying there thy golden head,
My pride in happier summers, at my feet.
The wrath which forced my thoughts on that fierce
       law,
The doom of treason and the flaming death
(When first I learnt thee hidden here), is past.
The pang—which while I weigh'd thy heart with one
Too wholly true to dream untruth in thee,
Made my tears burn—is also past—in part.
And all is past, the sin is sinn'd, and I,
Lo ! I forgive thee, as Eternal God
Forgives : do thou for thine own soul the rest.
But how to take last leave of all I loved ?
O golden hair, with which I used to play
Not knowing ! O imperial-moulded form,
And beauty such as never woman wore,
Until it came a kingdom's curse with thee—
I cannot touch thy lips, they are not mine,
But Lancelot's : nay, they never were the King's.
I cannot take thy hand ; that too is flesh,

And in the flesh thou hast sinn'd ; and mine own
    flesh,
Here looking down on thine polluted, cries,
' I loathe thee : ' yet not less, O Guinevere,
For I was ever virgin save for thee,
My love through flesh hath wrought into my life
So far, that my doom is, I love thee still.
Let no man dream but that I love thee still.
Perchance, and so thou purify thy soul,
And so thou lean on our fair Father Christ,
Hereafter in that world where all are pure
We two may meet before high God, and thou
Wilt spring to me, and claim me thine, and know
I am thine husband—not a smaller soul,
Nor Lancelot, nor another. Leave me that,
I charge thee, my last hope. Now must I hence.
Through the thick night I hear the trumpet blow :
They summon me their King to lead mine hosts
Far down to that great battle in the west,
Where I must strike against my sister's son,
Leagued with the Lords of the White Horse and
    knights
Once mine, and strike him dead, and meet myself
Death, or I know not what mysterious doom.
And thou remaining here wilt learn the event ;
But hither shall I never come again,
Never lie by thy side ; see thee no more—
Farewell ! "

        And while she grovell'd at his feet,
She felt the King's breath wander o'er her neck,
And in the darkness o'er her fallen head,
Perceived the waving of his hands that bless'd.

                    LORD TENNYSON.

ONE WORD MORE

TO E. B. B.

THERE they are, my fifty men and women
Naming me the fifty poems finished !
Take them, love, the book and me together :
Where the heart lies, let the brain lie also.

Rafael made a century of sonnets,
Made and wrote them in a certain volume
Dinted with the silver-pointed pencil
Else he only used to draw Madonnas :
These, the world might view—but one, the volume.
Who that one, you ask ?   Your heart instructs you.
Did she live and love it all her lifetime ?
Did she drop, his lady of the sonnets,
Die, and let it drop beside her pillow
Where it lay in place of Rafael's glory,
Rafael's cheek so duteous and so loving—
Cheek, the world was wont to hail a painter's,
Rafael's cheek, her love had turned a poet's ?

You and I would rather read that volume,
(Taken to his beating bosom by it)
Lean and list the bosom-beats of Rafael,
Would we not ? than wonder at Madonnas—
Her, San Sisto names, and Her, Foligno,
Her, that visits Florence in a vision,
Her, that's left with lilies in the Louvre—
Seen by us and all the world in circle.

You and I will never read that volume.
Guido Reni, like his own eye's apple
Guarded long the treasure-book and loved it.
Guido Reni dying, all Bologna

Cried, and the world cried too, " Ours, the treasure ! "
Suddenly, as rare things will, it vanished.

Dante once prepared to paint an angel :
Whom to please ?   You whisper " Beatrice."
While he mused and traced it and retraced it,
(Peradventure with a pen corroded
Still by drops of that hot ink he dipped for,
When, his left-hand i' the hair o' the wicked,
Back he held the brow and pricked its stigma,
Bit into the live man's flesh for parchment,
Loosed him, laughed to see the writing rankle,
Let the wretch go festering through Florence)—
Dante, who loved well because he hated,
Hated wickedness that hinders loving,
Dante standing, studying his angel,—
In there broke the folk of his Inferno.
Says he—" Certain people of importance "
(Such he gave his daily dreadful line to)
" Entered and would seize, forsooth, the poet."
Says the poet—" Then I stopped my painting."

You and I would rather see that angel,
Painted by the tenderness of Dante,
Would we not ?—than read a fresh Inferno.

You and I will never see that picture.
While he mused on love and Beatrice,
While he softened o'er his outlined angel,
In they broke, those " people of importance : "
We and Bice bear the loss for ever.

What of Rafael's sonnets, Dante's picture ?
This : no artist lives and loves, that longs not
Once, and only once, and for one only,
(Ah, the prize !) to find his love a language
Fit and fair and simple and sufficient—
Using nature that's an art to others,

II

Not, this one time, art that's turned his nature.
Ay, of all the artists living, loving,
None but would forego his proper dowry,—
Does he paint ? he fain would write a poem,—
Does he write ? he fain would paint a picture,
Put to proof art alien to the artist's,
Once, and only once, and for one only,
So to be the man and leave the artist,
Gain the man's joy, miss the artist's sorrow.

Wherefore ? Heaven's gift takes earth's abatement !
He who smites the rock and spreads the water,
Bidding drink and live a crowd beneath him,
Even he, the minute makes immortal,
Proves, perchance, but mortal in the minute,
Desecrates, belike, the deed in doing.
While he smites, how can he but remember,
So he smote before, in such a peril,
When they stood and mocked—" Shall smiting help
    us ? "
When they drank and sneered—" A stroke is easy ! "
When they wiped their mouths and went their journey,
Throwing him for thanks—" But drought was
    pleasant."
Thus old memories mar the actual triumph ;
Thus the doing savours of disrelish ;
Thus achievement lacks a gracious somewhat ;
O'er-importuned brows becloud the mandate,
Carelessness or consciousness—the gesture.
For he bears an ancient wrong about him,
Sees and knows again those phalanxed faces,
Hears, yet one time more, the 'customed prelude—
" How shouldst thou, of all men, smite, and save us ? "
Guesses what is like to prove the sequel—
" Egypt's flesh-pots—nay, the drought was better."

Oh, the crowd must have emphatic warrant !
Theirs, the Sinai-forehead's cloven brilliance,

Right-arm's rod-sweep, tongue's imperial fiat.
Never dares the man put off the prophet.

Did he love one face from out the thousands,
(Were she Jethro's daughter, white and wifely,
Were she but the Æthiopian bondslave,)
He would envy yon dumb patient camel,
Keeping a reserve of scanty water
Meant to save his own life in the desert ;
Ready in the desert to deliver
(Kneeling down to let his breast be opened)
Hoard and life together for his mistress.

I shall never, in the years remaining,
Paint you pictures, no, nor carve you statues,
Make you music that should all-express me ;
So it seems : I stand on my attainment.
This of verse alone, one life allows me ;
Verse and nothing else have I to give you
Other heights in other lives, God willing :
All the gifts from all the heights, your own, love !

Yet a semblance of resource avails us—
Shade so finely touched, love's sense must seize it.
Take these lines, look lovingly and nearly,
Lines I write the first time and the last time.
He who works in fresco, steals a hair-brush,
Curbs the liberal hand, subservient proudly,
Cramps his spirit, crowds its all in little,
Makes a strange art of an art familiar,
Fills his lady's missal-marge with flowerets.
He who blows thro' bronze, may breathe thro' silver,
Fitly serenade a slumbrous princess.
He who writes, may write for once as I do.

Love, you saw me gather men and women,
Live or dead or fashioned by my fancy,
Enter each and all, and use their service,

Speak from every mouth,—the speech, a poem.
Hardly shall I tell my joys and sorrows,
Hopes and fears, belief and disbelieving :
I am mine and yours—the rest be all men's,
Karshook, Cleon, Norbert and the fifty.
Let me speak this once in my true person,
Not as Lippo, Roland or Andrea,
Though the fruit of speech be just this sentence—
Pray you, look on these my men and women,
Take and keep my fifty poems finished ;
Where my heart lies, let my brain lie also !
Poor the speech ; be how I speak, for all things.

Not but that you know me ! Lo, the moon's self !
Here in London, yonder late in Florence,
Still we find her face, the thrice-transfigured.
Curving on a sky imbrued with colour,
Drifted over Fiesole by twilight,
Came she, our new crescent of a hair's-breadth.
Full she flared it, lamping Samminiato,
Rounder 'twixt the cypresses and rounder,
Perfect till the nightingales applauded.
Now, a piece of her old self, impoverished,
Hard to greet, she traverses the houseroofs,
Hurries with unhandsome thrift of silver,
Goes dispiritedly, glad to finish.

What, there's nothing in the moon note-worthy ?
Nay : for if that moon could love a mortal,
Use, to charm him (so to fit a fancy)
All her magic ('tis the old sweet mythos)
She would turn a new side to her mortal,
Side unseen of herdsman, huntsman, steersman—
Blank to Zoroaster on his terrace,
Blind to Galileo on his turret,
Dumb to Homer, dumb to Keats—him, even !
Think, the wonder of the moonstruck mortal—
When she turns round, comes again in heaven,

Opens out anew for worse or better!
Proves she like some portent of an iceberg
Swimming full upon the ship it founders,
Hungry with huge teeth of splintered crystals?
Proves she as the paved work of a sapphire
Seen by Moses when he climbed the mountain?
Moses, Aaron, Nadab and Abihu
Climbed and saw the very God, the Highest,
Stand upon the paved work of a sapphire.
Like the bodied heaven in his clearness
Shone the stone, the sapphire of that paved work,
When they ate and drank and saw God also!

What were seen? None knows, none ever shall know.
Only this is sure—the sight were other,
Not the moon's same side, born late in Florence,
Dying now impoverished here in London.
God be thanked, the meanest of his creatures
Boasts two soul-sides, one to face the world with,
One to show a woman when he loves her!

This I say of me, but think of you, love!
This to you—yourself my moon of poets!
Ah, but that's the world's side, there's the wonder,
Thus they see you, praise you, think they know you!
There, in turn I stand with them and praise you.
Out of my own self, I dare to phrase it.
But the best is when I glide from out them,
Cross a step or two of dubious twilight,
Come out on the other side, the novel
Silent silver lights and darks undreamed of,
Where I hush and bless myself with silence.

Oh, their Rafael of the dear Madonnas,
Oh, their Dante of the dread Inferno,
Wrote one song—and in my brain I sing it,
Drew one angel—borne, see, on my bosom!

ROBERT BROWNING.

PART V

POEMS OF FAITH

THE TWO VOICES

A STILL small voice spake unto me,
" Thou art so full of misery,
Were it not better not to be ? "

Then to the still small voice I said,
" Let me not cast in endless shade
What is so wonderfully made."

To which the voice did urge reply :
" To-day I saw the dragon-fly
Come from the wells where he did lie.

" An inner impulse rent the veil
Of his old husk : from head to tail
Came out clear plates of sapphire mail.

" He dried his wings : like gauze they grew :
Through crofts and pastures wet with dew
A living flash of light he flew."

I said, " When first the world began,
Young Nature through five cycles ran,
And in the sixth she moulded man.

" She gave him mind, the lordliest
Proportion, and, above the rest,
Dominion in the head and breast."

Thereto the silent voice replied :
" Self-blinded are you by your pride.
Look up through night : the world is wide.

" This truth within thy mind rehearse,
That in a boundless universe
Is boundless better, boundless worse.

" Think you this mould of hopes and fears
Could find no statelier than his peers
In yonder hundred million spheres ? "

It spake, moreover, in my mind :
" Though thou wert scatter'd to the wind,
Yet is there plenty of the kind."

Then did my response clearer fall :
" No compound of this earthly ball
Is like another, all in all."

To which he answer'd scoffingly :
" Good soul ! suppose I grant it thee,
Who'll weep for thy deficiency ?

" Or will one beam be less intense,
When the peculiar difference
Is cancell'd in the world of sense ? "

I would have said, " Thou canst not know."
But my full heart, that work'd below,
Rain'd through my sight its overflow.

Again the voice spake unto me :
" Thou art so steep'd in misery,
Surely 'twere better not to be.

" Thine anguish will not let thee sleep,
Nor any train of reason keep :
Thou canst not think, but thou wilt weep."

I said, " The years with change advance :
If I make dark my countenance,
I shut my life from happier chance.

" Some turn this sickness yet might take,
Ev'n yet."   But he : " What drug can make
A wither'd palsy cease to shake ? "

I wept, " Though I should die, I know
That all about the thorn will blow
In tufts of rosy-tinted snow ;

" And men, through novel spheres of thought
Still moving after truth long sought,
Will learn new things when I am not."

" Yet," said the secret voice, " some time,
Sooner or later, will grey prime
Make thy grass hoar with early rime.

" Not less swift souls that yearn for light,
Rapt after heaven's starry flight,
Would sweep the tracts of day and night.

" Not less the bee would range her cells,
The furzy prickle fire the dells,
The foxglove cluster dappled bells."

I said that " all the years invent ;
Each month is various to present
The world with some development.

" Were this not well, to bide mine hour
Though watching from a ruin'd tower
How grows the day of human power ? "

" The highest-mounted mind," he said,
" Still sees the sacred morning spread
The silent summit overhead.

" Will thirty seasons render plain
Those lonely lights that still remain,
Just breaking over land and main ?

" Or make that morn, from his cold crown
And crystal silence creeping down,
Flood with full daylight glebe and town ?

" Forerun thy peers, thy time, and let
Thy feet, millenniums hence, be set
In midst of knowledge, dream'd not yet.

" Thou hast not gain'd a real height,
Nor art thou nearer to the light,
Because the scale is infinite.

" 'Twere better not to breathe or speak,
Than cry for stength, remaining weak,
And seem to find, but still to seek.

" Moreover, but to seem to find
Asks what thou lackest, thought resign'd,
A healthy frame, a quiet mind."

I said, " When I am gone away,
' He dared not tarry,' men will say,
Doing dishonour to my clay."

" This is more vile," he made reply,
" To breathe and loathe, to live and sigh,
Than once from dread of pain to die.

" Sick art thou—a divided will
Still heaping on the fear of ill
The fear of men, a coward still.

" Do men love thee ? Art thou so bound
To men that how thy name may sound
Will vex thee lying underground ?

" The memory of the wither'd leaf
In endless time is scarce more brief
Than of the garner'd autumn-sheaf.

" Go, vexed Spirit, sleep in trust ;
The right ear, that is fill'd with dust,
Hears little of the false or just."

" Hard task, to pluck resolve," I cried,
" From emptiness and the waste wide
Of that abyss, or scornful pride !

" Nay—rather yet that I could raise
One hope that warm'd me in the days
While still I yearn'd for human praise.

" When, wide in soul and bold of tongue,
Among the tents I paused and sung,
The distant battle flash'd and rung.

" I sung the joyful Pæan clear,
And, sitting, burnish'd without fear
The brand, the buckler, and the spear—

" Waiting to strive a happy strife,
To war with falsehood to the knife,
And not to lose the good of life—

" Some hidden principle to move,
To put together, part and prove,
And mete the bounds of hate and love—

" As far as might be, to carve out
Free space for every human doubt,
That the whole mind might orb about—

" To search through all I felt or saw,
The springs of life, the depths of awe,
And reach the law within the law :

" At least, not rotting like a weed,
But, having sown some generous seed,
Fruitful of further thought and deed,

" To pass, when Life her light withdraws,
Not void of righteous self-applause,
Nor in a merely selfish cause—

" In some good cause, not in mine own,
To perish, wept for, honour'd, known,
And like a warrior overthrown ;

" Whose eyes are dim with glorious tears,
When, soil'd with noble dust, he hears
His country's war-song thrill his ears :

" Then dying of a mortal stroke,
What time the foeman's line is broke,
And all the war is roll'd in smoke."

" Yea ! " said the voice, " thy dream was good,
While thou abodest in the bud.
It was the stirring of the blood.

" If Nature put not forth her power
About the opening of the flower,
Who is it that could live an hour ?

" Then comes the check, the change, the fall.
Pain rises up, old pleasures pall.
There is one remedy for all.

" Yet hadst thou, through enduring pain,
Link'd month to month with such a chain
Of knitted purport, all were vain.

" Thou hadst not between death and birth
Dissolved the riddle of the earth.
So were thy labour little worth.

" That men with knowledge merely play'd,
I told thee—hardly nigher made,
Though scaling slow from grade to grade :

" Much less this dreamer, deaf and blind,
Named man, may hope some truth to find,
That bears relation to the mind.

" For every worm beneath the moon
Draws different threads, and late and soon
Spins, toiling out his own cocoon.

" Cry, faint not : either Truth is born
Beyond the polar gleam forlorn,
Or in the gateways of the morn.

' Cry, faint not, climb : the summits slope
Beyond the furthest flights of hope,
Wrapt in dense cloud from base to cope.

" Sometimes a little corner shines,
As over rainy mist inclines
A gleaming crag with belts of pines.

" I will go forward, sayest thou,
I shall not fail to find her now.
Look up, the fold is on her brow.

" If straight thy track, or if oblique,
Thou know'st not. Shadows thou dost strike,
Embracing cloud, Ixion-like ;

" And owning but a little more
Than beasts, abidest lame and poor,
Calling thyself a little lower

" Than angels. Cease to wail and brawl !
Why inch by inch to darkness crawl ?
There is one remedy for all."

" O dull, one-sided voice," said I,
" Wilt thou make everything a lie,
To flatter me that I may die ?

" I know that age to age succeeds,
Blowing a noise of tongues and deeds,
A dust of systems and of creeds.

" I cannot hide that some have striven,
Achieving calm, to whom was given
The joy that mixes man with Heaven :

" Who, rowing hard against the stream,
Saw distant gates of Eden gleam,
And did not dream it was a dream ;

" But heard, by secret transport led,
Ev'n in the charnels of the dead,
The murmur of the fountain-head—

" Which did accomplish their desire,
Bore and forbore, and did not tire,
Like Stephen, an unquenched fire.

" He heeded not reviling tones,
Nor sold his heart to idle moans,
Though cursed and scorn'd, and bruised with stones:

" But looking upward, full of grace,
He pray'd, and from a happy place
God's glory smote him on the face."

The sullen answer slid betwixt :
" Not that the grounds of hope were fix'd,
The elements were kindlier mix'd."

I said, " I toil beneath the curse,
But, knowing not the universe,
I fear to slide from bad to worse.

" And that, in seeking to undo
One riddle, and to find the true,
I knit a hundred others new :

" Or that this anguish fleeting hence,
Unmanacled from bonds of sense,
Be fix'd and froz'n to permanence :

" For I go, weak from suffering here ;
Naked I go, and void of cheer :
What is it that I may not fear ? "

" Consider well," the voice replied,
" His face, that two hours since hath died ;
Wilt thou find passion, pain or pride ?

" Will he obey when one commands ?
Or answer should one press his hands ?
He answers not, nor understands.

" His palms are folded on his breast :
There is no other thing express'd
But long disquiet merged in rest.

" His lips are very mild and meek :
Though one should smite him on the cheek,
And on the mouth, he will not speak.

" His little daughter, whose sweet face
He kiss'd, taking his last embrace,
Becomes dishonour to her race ;

" His sons grow up that bear his name,
Some grow to honour, some to shame,—
But he is chill to praise or blame.

" He will not hear the north wind rave,
Nor, moaning, household shelter crave
From winter rains that beat his grave.

" High up the vapours fold and swim :
About him broods the twilight dim :
The place he knew forgetteth him."

" If all be dark, vague voice," I said,
" These things are wrapt in doubt and dread,
Nor canst thou show the dead are dead.

" The sap dries up : the plant declines.
A deeper tale my heart divines.
Know I not Death ? the outward signs ?

" I found him when my years were few ;
A shadow on the graves I knew,
And darkness in the village yew.

" From grave to grave the shadow crept :
In her still place the morning wept :
Touch'd by his feet the daisy slept.

" The simple senses crown'd his head :
' Omega ! thou art Lord,' they said,
' We find no motion in the dead.'

" Why, if man rot in dreamless ease,
Should that plain fact, as taught by these,
Not make him sure that he shall cease ?

" Who forged that other influence,
That heat of inward evidence,
By which he doubts against the sense ?

" He owns the fatal gift of eyes,
That read his spirit blindly wise,
Not simple as a thing that dies.

" Here sits he shaping wings to fly :
His heart forebodes a mystery :
He names the name Eternity.

" That type of Perfect in his mind
In Nature can he nowhere find.
He sows himself on every wind.

" He seems to hear a Heavenly Friend,
And through thick veils to apprehend
A labour working to an end.

" The end and the beginning vex
His reason ; many things perplex,
With motions, checks, and counter-checks.

" He knows a baseness in his blood
At such strange war with something good,
He may not do the thing he would.

" Heaven opens inward, chasms yawn,
Vast images in glimmering dawn,
Half shown, are broken and withdrawn.

" Ah ! sure within him and without,
Could his dark wisdom find it out,
There must be answer to his doubt.

" But thou canst answer not again.
With thine own weapon art thou slain,
Or thou wilt answer but in vain.

" The doubt would rest, I dare not solve.
In the same circle we revolve.
Assurance only breeds resolve."

As when a billow, blown against,
Falls back, the voice with which I fenced
A little ceased, but recommenced :

" Where wert thou when thy father play'd
In his free field, and pastime made,
A merry boy in sun and shade ?

" A merry boy they called him then.
He sat upon the knees of men
In days that never come again,

" Before the little ducts began
To feed thy bones with lime, and ran
Their course, till thou wert also man :

" Who took a wife, who rear'd his race,
Whose wrinkles gather'd on his face,
Whose troubles number with his days :

" A life of nothings, nothing-worth,
From that first nothing ere his birth
To that last nothing under earth ! "

" These words," I said, " are like the rest ;
No certain clearness, but at best
A vague suspicion of the breast :

" But if I grant, thou mightst defend
The thesis which thy words intend—
That to begin implies to end ;

" Yet how should I for certain hold,
Because my memory is so cold,
That I first was in human mould ?

" I cannot make this matter plain,
But I would shoot, howe'er in vain,
A random arrow from the brain.

" It may be that no life is found,
Which only to one engine bound
Falls off, but cycles always round.

(2,599)

" As old mythologies relate,
Some draught of Lethe might await
The slipping through from state to state.

" As here we find in trances, men
Forget the dream that happens then,
Until they fall in trance again.

" So might we, if our state were such
As one before, remember much,
For those two likes might meet and touch.

" But, if I lapsed from nobler place,
Some legend of a fallen race
Alone might hint of my disgrace ;

" Some vague emotion of delight
In gazing up an Alpine height,
Some yearning toward the lamps of night.

" Or if through lower lives I came—
Though all experience past became
Consolidate in mind and frame—

" I might forget my weaker lot ;
For is not our first year forgot ?
The haunts of memory echo not.

" And men, whose reason long was blind,
From cells of madness unconfined,
Oft lose whole years of darker mind.

" Much more, if first I floated free,
As naked essence, must I be
Incompetent of memory :

" For memory dealing but with time,
And he with matter, could she climb
Beyond her own material prime ?

" Moreover, something is or seems,
That touches me with mystic gleams,
Like glimpses of forgotten dreams—

" Of something felt, like something here ;
Of something done, I know not where ;
Such as no language may declare."

The still voice laugh'd. " I talk," said he,
" Not with thy dreams. Suffice it thee
Thy pain is a reality."

" But thou," said I, " hast miss'd thy mark,
Who sought'st to wreck my mortal ark,
By making all the horizon dark.

" Why not set forth, if I should do
This rashness, that which might ensue
With this old soul in organs new ?

" Whatever crazy sorrow saith,
No life that breathes with human breath
Has ever truly long'd for death.

" 'Tis life, whereof our nerves are scant,
Oh life, not death, for which we pant ;
More life, and fuller, that I want."

I ceased, and sat as one forlorn.
Then said the voice, in quiet scorn,
" Behold, it is the Sabbath morn."

And I arose, and I released
The casement, and the light increased
With freshness in the dawning east.

Like soften'd airs that blowing steal,
When meres begin to uncongeal,
The sweet church bells began to peal.

On to God's house the people prest :
Passing the place where each must rest,
Each enter'd like a welcome guest.

One walk'd between his wife and child,
With measured footfall firm and mild,
And now and then he gravely smiled.

The prudent partner of his blood
Lean'd on him, faithful, gentle, good,
Wearing the rose of womanhood.

And in their double love secure,
The little maiden walk'd demure,
Pacing with downward eyelids pure.

These three made unity so sweet,
My frozen heart began to beat,
Remembering its ancient heat.

I blest them, and they wander'd on :
I spoke, but answer came there none :
The dull and bitter voice was gone.

A second voice was at mine ear,
A little whisper silver-clear,
A murmur, " Be of better cheer."

As from some blissful neighbourhood,
A notice faintly understood,
" I see the end, and know the good."

A little hint to solace woe,
A hint, a whisper breathing low,
" I may not speak of what I know."

Like an Æolian harp that wakes
No certain air, but overtakes
Far thought with music that it makes,

Such seem'd the whisper at my side :
" What is it thou knowest, sweet voice ? " I cried.
" A hidden hope," the voice replied :

So heavenly-toned, that in that hour
From out my sullen heart a power
Broke, like the rainbow from the shower,

To feel, although no tongue can prove,
That every cloud, that spreads above
And veileth love, itself is love.

And forth into the fields I went,
And Nature's living motion lent
The pulse of hope to discontent.

I wonder'd at the bounteous hours,
The slow result of winter showers :
You scarce could see the grass for flowers.

I wonder'd, while I paced along :
The woods were fill'd so full with song,
There seem'd no room for sense of wrong.

So variously seem'd all things wrought,
I marvell'd how the mind was brought
To anchor by one gloomy thought ;

And wherefore rather I made choice
To commune with that barren voice,
Than him that said, " Rejoice ! rejoice ! "

LORD TENNYSON.

PIPPA'S SONG

(*From " Pippa Passes "*)

[A girl, Pippa, from the silk-mills, on her New Year's
Day holiday, passes through the streets of Asolo, singing snatches of song which convert those who hear her.]

THE year's at the spring,
And day's at the morn ;
Morning's at seven ;
The hill-side's dew-pearled ;
The larks on the wing ;
The snail's on the thorn :
God's in his heaven—
All's right with the world !

ROBERT BROWNING.

ST. AGNES' EVE

DEEP on the convent-roof the snows
    Are sparkling to the moon :
My breath to heaven like vapour goes :
    May my soul follow soon !
The shadows of the convent-towers
    Slant down the snowy sward,
Still creeping with the creeping hours
    That lead me to my Lord :
Make Thou my spirit pure and clear
    As are the frosty skies,
Or this first snowdrop of the year
    That in my bosom lies.

As these white robes are soil'd and dark,
  To yonder shining ground ;
As this pale taper's earthly spark,
  To yonder argent round ;
So shows my soul before the Lamb,
  My spirit before Thee :
So in mine earthly house I am,
  To that I hope to be.
Break up the heavens, O Lord ! and far,
  Through all yon starlight keen,
Draw me, thy bride, a glittering star,
  In raiment white and clean.

He lifts me to the golden doors ;
  The flashes come and go ;
All heaven bursts her starry floors,
  And strows her lights below,
And deepens on and up ! the gates
  Roll back, and far within
For me the Heavenly Bridegroom waits,
  To make me pure of sin.
The sabbaths of Eternity,
  One sabbath deep and wide—
A light upon the shining sea—
  The Bridegroom with his bride !
LORD TENNYSON.

THE BOY AND THE ANGEL

MORNING, evening, noon and night,
" Praise God ! " sang Theocrite.

Then to his poor trade he turned,
Whereby the daily meal was earned.

Hard he laboured, long and well ;
O'er his work the boy's curls fell.

But ever, at each period,
He stopped and sang, " Praise God ! "

Then back again his curls he threw,
And cheerful turned to work anew.

Said Blaise, the listening monk, " Well done ;
I doubt not thou art heard, my son :

" As well as if thy voice to-day
Were praising God, the Pope's great way.

" This Easter Day, the Pope at Rome
Praises God from Peter's dome."

Said Theocrite, " Would God that I
Might praise him, that great way, and die ! "

Night passed, day shone,
And Theocrite was gone.

With God a day endures alway,
A thousand years are but a day.

God said in heaven, " Nor day nor night
Now brings the voice of my delight."

Then Gabriel, like a rainbow's birth,
Spread his wings and sank to earth ;

Entered, in flesh, the empty cell,
Lived there, and played the craftsman well ;

And morning, evening, noon and night,
Praised God in place of Theocrite.

And from a boy, to youth he grew :
The man put off the stripling's hue :

The man matured and fell away
Into the season of decay :

And ever o'er the trade he bent,
And ever lived on earth content.

(He did God's will ; to him, all one
If on the earth or in the sun.)

God said, " A praise is in mine ear ;
There is no doubt in it, no fear :

" So sing old worlds, and so
New worlds that from my footstool go.

" Clearer loves sound other ways :
I miss my little human praise."

Then forth sprang Gabriel's wings, off fell
The flesh disguise, remained the cell.

'Twas Easter Day : he flew to Rome,
And paused above Saint Peter's dome.

In the tiring-room close by
The great outer gallery,

With his holy vestments dight,
Stood the new Pope, Theocrite :

And all his past career
Came back upon him clear,

Since when, a boy, he plied his trade,
Till on his life the sickness weighed;

And in his cell, when death drew near,
An angel in a dream brought cheer:

And rising from the sickness drear
He grew a priest, and now stood here.

To the East with praise he turned,
And on his sight the angel burned.

" I bore thee from thy craftsman's cell,
And set thee here; I did not well.

" Vainly I left my angel-sphere,
Vain was thy dream of many a year.

" Thy voice's praise seemed weak; it dropped—
Creation's chorus stopped!

" Go back and praise again
The early way, while I remain.

" With that weak voice of our disdain,
Take up creation's pausing strain.

" Back to the cell and poor employ:
Resume the craftsman and the boy! "

Theocrite grew old at home;
A new Pope dwelt in Peter's dome.

One vanished as the other died:
They sought God side by side.

ROBERT BROWNING.

SAUL

I

SAID Abner, " At last thou art come !   Ere I tell, ere thou speak,

Kiss my cheek, wish me well ! "   Then I wished it, and did kiss his cheek.

And he, " Since the King, O my friend, for thy countenance sent,

Neither drunken nor eaten have we ; nor until from his tent

Thou return with the joyful assurance the King liveth yet,

Shall our lip with the honey be bright, with the water be wet.

For out of the black mid-tent's silence, a space of three days,

Not a sound hath escaped to thy servants, of prayer nor of praise,

To betoken that Saul and the Spirit have ended their strife,

And that, faint in his triumph, the monarch sinks back upon life

II

" Yet now my heart leaps, O beloved !   God's child with his dew

On thy gracious gold hair, and those lilies still living and blue

Just broken to twine round thy harp-strings, as if no wild heat

Were now raging to torture the desert ! "

III

Then I, as was meet,
Knelt down to the God of my fathers, and rose on my
feet,
And ran o'er the sand burnt to powder.   The tent was
unlooped ;
I pulled up the spear that obstructed, and under I
stooped ;
Hands and knees on the slippery grass-patch, all
withered and gone,
That extends to the second enclosure, I groped my
way on
Till I felt where the foldskirts fly open.   Then once
more I prayed,
And opened the foldskirts and entered, and was not
afraid
But spoke, " Here is David, thy servant ! "   And no
voice replied.
At the first I saw nought but the blackness ; but soon
I descried
A something more black than the blackness—the vast,
the upright
Main prop which sustains the pavilion : and slow into
sight
Grew a figure against it, gigantic and blackest of all.
Then a sunbeam, that burst thro' the tent-roof, showed
Saul.

IV

He stood as erect as that tent-prop, both arms
stretched out wide
On the great cross-support in the centre, that goes to
each side ;
He relaxed not a muscle, but hung there as, caught in
his pangs
And waiting his change, the king-serpent all heavily
hangs,

Far away from his kind, in the pine, till deliverance
come
With the spring-time,—so agonized Saul, drear and
stark, blind and dumb.

v

Then I tuned my harp,—took off the lilies we twine
round its chords
Lest they snap 'neath the stress of the noontide—
those sunbeams like swords !
And I first played the tune all our sheep know, as, one
after one,
So docile they come to the pen-door till folding be
done.
They are white and untorn by the bushes, for lo, they
have fed
Where the long grasses stifle the water within the
stream's bed ;
And now one after one seeks its lodging, as star follows
star
Into eve and the blue far above us,—so blue and so far !

VI

—Then the tune, for which quails on the cornland will
each leave his mate
To fly after the player ; then, what makes the crickets
elate
Till for boldness they fight one another : and then,
what has weight
To set the quick jerboa a-musing outside his sand
house—
There are none such as he for a wonder, half bird
and half mouse !
God made all the creatures and gave them our love
and our fear,
To give sign, we and they are his children, one family
here.

VII

Then I played the help-tune of our reapers, their wine-
song, when hand
Grasps at hand, eye lights eye in good friendship, and
great hearts expand
And grow one in the sense of this world's life.—And
then, the last song
When the dead man is praised on his journey—" Bear,
bear him along
With his few faults shut up like dead flowerets !   Are
balm seeds not here
To console us ?   The land has none left such as he on
the bier.
Oh, would we might keep thee, my brother ! "—And
then, the glad chaunt
Of the marriage,—first go the young maidens, next,
she whom we vaunt
As the beauty, the pride of our dwelling.—And then,
the great march
Wherein man runs to man to assist him and buttress
an arch
Nought can break ; who shall harm them, our friends?
—Then, the chorus intoned
As the levites go up to the altar in glory enthroned.
But I stopped here : for here in the darkness Saul
groaned.

VIII

And I paused, held my breath in such silence, and
listened apart ;
And the tent shook, for mighty Saul shuddered : and
sparkles 'gan dart
From the jewels that woke in his turban at once with
a start,
All its lordly male-sapphires, and rubies courageous
at heart.

So the head : but the body still moved not, still hung
    there erect.

And I bent once again to my playing, pursued it
    unchecked,

As I sang,

IX

        " Oh, our manhood's prime vigour ! No
  spirit feels waste,

Not a muscle is stopped in its playing nor sinew un-
    braced.

Oh, the wild joys of living ! the leaping from rock up
    to rock,

The strong rending of boughs from the fir-tree, the
    cool silver shock

Of the plunge in a pool's living water, the hunt of the
    bear,

And the sultriness showing the lion is couched in his lair,

And the meal, the rich dates yellowed over with gold
    dust divine,

And the locust-flesh steeped in the pitcher, the full
    draught of wine,

And the sleep in the dried river-channel where bul-
    rushes tell

That the water was wont to go warbling so softly and
    well.

How good is man's life, the mere living ! how fit to
    employ

All the heart and the soul and the senses for ever in
    joy !

Hast thou loved the white locks of thy father, whose
    sword thou didst guard

When he trusted thee forth with the armies, for glori-
    ous reward ?

Didst thou see the thin hands of thy mother, held up
    as men sung

The low song of the nearly-departed, and hear her
    faint tongue

Joining in while it could to the witness, ' Let one
    more attest,
I have lived, seen God's hand thro' a lifetime, and all
    was for best ! '
Then they sung thro' their tears in strong triumph,
    not much, but the rest.
And thy brothers, the help and the contest, the work-
    ing whence grew
Such result as, from seething grape-bundles, the spirit
    strained true :
And the friends of thy boyhood—that boyhood of
    wonder and hope,
Present promise and wealth of the future beyond the
    eye's scope,—
Till lo, thou art grown to a monarch ; a people is
    thine ;
And all gifts, which the world offers singly, on one
    head combine !
On one head, all the beauty and strength, love and
    rage (like the throe
That, a-work in the rock, helps its labour and lets the
    gold go)
High ambition and deeds which surpass it, fame
    crowning them,—all
Brought to blaze on the head of one creature—King
    Saul ! ''

X

And lo, with that leap of my spirit,—heart, hand,
    harp and voice,
Each lifting Saul's name out of sorrow, each bidding
    rejoice
Saul's fame in the light it was made for—as when,
    dare I say,
The Lord's army, in rapture of service, strains through
    its array,
And upsoareth the cherubim-chariot—" Saul ! " cried
    I, and stopped,

And waited the thing that should follow. Then Saul,
  who hung propped
By the tent's cross-support in the centre, was struck
  by his name.
Have ye seen when Spring's arrowy summons goes
  right to the aim,
And some mountain, the last to withstand her, that
  held (he alone,
While the vale laughed in freedom and flowers) on a
  broad bust of stone
A year's snow bound about for a breastplate,—leaves
  grasp of the sheet ?
Fold on fold all at once it crowds thunderously down
  to his feet,
And there fronts you, stark, black, but alive yet, your
  mountain of old,
With his rents, the successive bequeathings of ages
  untold—
Yea, each harm got in fighting your battles, each
  furrow and scar
Of his head thrust 'twixt you and the tempest—all
  hail, there they are !
—Now again to be softened with verdure, again hold
  the nest
Of the dove, tempt the goat and its young to the green
  on his crest
For their food in the ardours of summer. One long
  shudder thrilled
All the tent till the very air tingled, then sank and
  was stilled
At the King's self left standing before me, released and
  aware.
What was gone, what remained ? All to traverse
  'twixt hope and despair.
Death was past, life not come : so he waited. Awhile
  his right hand
Held the brow, helped the eyes left too vacant forth-
  with to remand

(2,599)

To their place what new objects should enter :   twas
    Saul as before.
I looked up and dared gaze at those eyes, nor was hurt
    any more
Than by slow pallid sunsets in autumn, ye watch from
    the shore,
At their sad level gaze o'er the ocean—a sun's slow
    decline
Over hills which, resolved in stern silence, o'erlap and
    entwine
Base with base to knit strength more intensely : so,
    arm folded arm
O'er the chest whose slow heavings subsided.

XI

                 What spell or what charm,
(For, awhile there was trouble within me) what next
    should I urge
To sustain him where song had restored him ?—Song
    filled to the verge
His cup with the wine of this life, pressing all that it
    yields
Of mere fruitage, the strength and the beauty : be-
    yond, on what fields,
Glean a vintage more potent and perfect to brighten
    the eye
And bring blood to the lip, and commend them the cup
    they put by ?
He saith, " It is good ; " still he drinks not : he lets
    me praise life,
Gives assent, yet would die for his own part.

XII

                 Then fancies grew rife
Which had come long ago on the pasture, when round
    me the sheep

Fed in silence—above, the one eagle wheeled slow as
    in sleep ;

And I lay in my hollow and mused on the world that
    might lie

'Neath his ken, though I saw but the strip 'twixt the
    hill and the sky :

And I laughed—" Since my days are ordained to be
    passed with my flocks,

Let me people at least, with my fancies, the plains
    and the rocks,

Dream the life I am never to mix with, and image the
    show

Of mankind as they live in those fashions I hardly
    shall know !

Schemes of life, its best rules and right uses, the
    courage that gains,

And the prudence that keeps what men strive for."
    And now these old trains

Of vague thought came again ; I grew surer ; so, once
    more the string

Of my harp made response to my spirit, as thus—

XIII

                      " Yea, my King,"

I began—" thou dost well in rejecting mere comforts
    that spring

From the mere mortal life held in common by man
    and by brute :

In our flesh grows the branch of this life, in our soul
    it bears fruit.

Thou hast marked the slow rise of the tree,—how its
    stem trembled first

Till it passed the kid's lip, the stag's antler ; then
    safely outburst

The fan-branches all round ; and thou mindedst when
    these too, in turn

Broke a-bloom and the palm-tree seemed perfect :
    yet more was to learn,

E'en the good that comes in with the palm-fruit.   Our
    dates shall we slight,
When their juice brings a cure for all sorrow ? or care
    for the plight
Of the palm's self whose slow growth produced them ?
    Not so ! stem and branch
Shall decay, nor be known in their place, while the
    palm-wine shall staunch
Every wound of man's spirit in winter.   I pour thee
    such wine.
Leave the flesh to the fate it was fit for ! the spirit
    be thine !
By the spirit, when age shall o'ercome thee, thou still
    shalt enjoy
More indeed, than at first when inconscious, the life of
    a boy.
Crush that life, and behold its wine running ! Each
    deed thou hast done
Dies, revives, goes to work in the world ; until e'en as
    the sun
Looking down on the earth, though clouds spoil him,
    though tempests efface,
Can find nothing his own deed produced not, must
    everywhere trace
The results of his past summer-prime,—so, each ray
    of thy will,
Every flash of thy passion and prowess, long over,
    shall thrill
Thy whole people the countless, with ardour, till they
    too give forth
A like cheer to their sons, who in turn, fill the South
    and the North
With radiance thy deed was the germ of.   Carouse
    in the past !
But the license of age has its limit ; thou diest at
    last :
As the lion when age dims his eyeball, the rose at her
    height,

So with man—so his power and his beauty for ever
    take flight.
No ! Again a long draught of my soul-wine ! Look
    forth o'er the years !
Thou hast done now with eyes for the actual; begin
    with the seer's !
Is Saul dead ? In the depth of the vale make his tomb
    —bid arise
A grey mountain of marble heaped four-square, till,
    built to the skies,
Let it mark where the great First King slumbers :
    whose fame would ye know ?
Up above see the rock's naked face, where the record
    shall go
In great characters cut by the scribe,—Such was Saul,
    so he did ;
With the sages directing the work, by the populace
    chid,—
For not half, they'll affirm, is comprised there ! Which
    fault to amend,
In the grove with his kind grows the cedar, whereon
    they shall spend
(See, in tablets 'tis level before them) their praise,
    and record
With the gold of the graver, Saul's story,—the states-
    man's great word
Side by side with the poet's sweet comment. The
    river's a-wave
With smooth paper-reeds grazing each other when
    prophet-winds rave :
So the pen gives unborn generations their due and
    their part
In thy being ! Then, first of the mighty, thank God
    that thou art ! "

XIV

And behold while I sang . . . but O Thou who didst
    grant me that day,

And before it not seldom hast granted thy help to
  essay,
Carry on and complete an adventure,—my shield and
  my sword
In that act where my soul was thy servant, thy word
  was my word,—
Still be with me, who then at the summit of human
  endeavour
And scaling the highest, man's thought could, gazed
  hopeless as ever
On the new stretch of heaven above me—till, mighty
  to save,
Just one lift of thy hand cleared that distance—God's
  throne from man's grave !
Let me tell out my tale to its ending—my voice to my
  heart
Which can scarce dare believe in what marvels last
  night I took part,
As this morning I gather the fragments, alone with my
  sheep,
And still fear lest the terrible glory evanish like sleep !
For I wake in the grey dewy covert, while Hebron
  upheaves
The dawn struggling with night on his shoulder, and
  Kidron retrieves
Slow the damage of yesterday's sunshine.

XV

                          I say then,—my song
While I sang thus, assuring the monarch, and ever
  more strong
Made a proffer of good to console him—he slowly
  resumed
His old motions and habitudes kingly. The right hand
  replumed
His black locks to their wonted composure, adjusted
  the swathes

Of his turban, and see—the huge sweat that his coun-
tenance bathes,
He wipes off with the robe ; and he girds now his loins
as of yore,
And feels slow for the armlets of price, with the clasp
set before.
He is Saul, ye remember in glory,—ere error had
bent
The broad brow from the daily communion ; and still,
though much spent
Be the life and the bearing that front you, the same,
God did choose,
To receive what a man may waste, desecrate, never
quite lose.
So sank he along by the tent-prop till, stayed by the
pile
Of his armour and war-cloak and garments, he leaned
there awhile,
And sat out my singing,—one arm round the tent-prop,
to raise
His bent head, and the other hung slack—till I touched
on the praise
I foresaw from all men in all time, to the man patient
there ;
And thus ended, the harp falling forward. Then first
I was 'ware
That he sat, as I say, with my head just above his vast
knees
Which were thrust out on each side around me, like
oak roots which please
To encircle a lamb when it slumbers. I looked up to
know
If the best I could do had brought solace : he spoke
not, but slow
Lifted up the hand slack at his side, till he laid it with
care
Soft and grave, but in mild settled will, on my brow :
thro' my hair

The large fingers were pushed, and he bent back my
    head, with kind power—
All my face back, intent to peruse it, as men do a
    flower.
Thus held he me there with his great eyes that scruti-
    nized mine—
And oh, all my heart how it loved him ! but where was
    the sign ?
I yearned—" Could I help thee, my father, inventing
    a bliss,
I would add, to that life of the past, both the future
    and this ;
I would give thee new life altogether, as good, ages
    hence,
As this moment,—had love but the warrant, love's
    heart to dispense ! "

XVI

Then the truth came upon me. No harp more—no
    song more ! out-broke—

XVII

" I have gone the whole round of creation : I saw
    and I spoke :
I, a work of God's hand for that purpose, received in
    my brain
And pronounced on the rest of his handwork—re-
    turned him again
His creation's approval or censure : I spoke as I saw.
I report, as a man may of God's work—all's love, yet
    all's law.
Now I lay down the judgeship he lent me. Each
    faculty tasked
To perceive him, has gained an abyss, where a dew-
    drop was asked.
Have I knowledge ? confounded it shrivels at Wisdom
    laid bare.

Have I forethought ? how purblind, how blank, to the
    Infinite Care !
Do I task any faculty highest, to image success ?
I but open my eyes,—and perfection, no more and no
    less,
In the kind I imagined, full-fronts me, and God is
    seen God
In the star, in the stone, in the flesh, in the soul and
    the clod.
And thus looking within and around me, I ever renew
(With that stoop of the soul which in bending up-
    raises it too)
The submission of man's nothing-perfect to God's all-
    complete,
As by each new obeisance in spirit, I climb to his feet.
Yet with all this abounding experience, this deity
    known,
I shall dare to discover some province, some gift of my
    own.
There's a faculty pleasant to exercise, hard to hood-
    wink,
I am fain to keep still in abeyance, (I laugh as I
    think)
Lest, insisting to claim and parade in it, wot ye, I
    worst
E'en the Giver in one gift.—Behold, I could love if
    I durst !
But I sink the pretension as fearing a man may o'er-
    take
God's own speed in the one way of love : I abstain for
    love's sake.
—What, my soul ? see thus far and no farther ? when
    doors great and small,
Nine-and-ninety flew ope at our touch, should the
    hundredth appal ?
In the least things have faith, yet distrust in the
    greatest of all ?
Do I find love so full in my nature, God's ultimate gift,

That I doubt his own love can compete with it ?
    Here, the parts shift ?
Here, the creature surpass the Creator,—the end, what
    Began ?
Would I fain in my impotent yearning do all for this
    man,
And dare doubt he alone shall not help him, who yet
    alone can ?
Would it ever have entered my mind, the bare will,
    much less power,
To bestow on this Saul what I sang of, the marvellous
    dower
Of the life he was gifted and filled with ? to make such
    a soul,
Such a body, and then such an earth for insphering
    the whole ?
And doth it not enter my mind (as my warm tears
    attest)
These good things being given, to go on, and give one
    more, the best ?
Ay, to save and redeem and restore him, maintain at
    the height
This perfection,—succeed with life's dayspring, death's
    minute of night ?
Interpose at the difficult minute, snatch Saul, the
    mistake,
Saul, the failure, the ruin he seems now,—and bid
    him awake
From the dream, the probation, the prelude, to find
    himself set
Clear and safe in new light and new life,—a new
    harmony yet
To be run, and continued, and ended—who knows ?
    —or endure !
The man taught enough by life's dream, of the rest to
    make sure ;
By the pain-throb, triumphantly winning intensified
    bliss,

And the next world's reward and repose, by the
struggles in this.

XVIII

" I believe it ! 'Tis thou, God, that givest, 'tis I who
receive :
In the first is the last, in thy will is my power to
believe.
All's one gift : thou canst grant it moreover, as
prompt to my prayer
As I breathe out this breath, as I open these arms to
the air.
From thy will, stream the worlds, life and nature, thy
dread Sabaoth :
I will ?—the mere atoms despise me ! Why am I not
loth
To look that, even that in the face too ? Why is it I
dare
Think but lightly of such impuissance ? What stops
my despair ?
This ;—'tis not what man Does which exalts him, but
what man Would do !
See the King—I would help him but cannot, the
wishes fall through.
Could I wrestle to raise him from sorrow, grow poor to
enrich,
To fill up his life, starve my own out, I would—knowing which,
I know that my service is perfect. Oh, speak through
me now !
Would I suffer for him that I love ? So wouldst thou
—so wilt thou !
So shall crown thee the topmost, ineffablest, uttermost
crown—
And thy love fill infinitude wholly, nor leave up nor
down
One spot for the creature to stand in ! It is by no
breath,

Turn of eye, wave of hand, that salvation joins issue
    with death !
As thy Love is discovered almighty, almighty be proved
Thy power, that exists with and for it, of being
    Beloved !
He who did most, shall bear most ; the strongest shall
    stand the most weak.
'Tis the weakness in strength, that I cry for ! my
    flesh, that I seek
In the Godhead ! I seek and I find it. O Saul, it
    shall be
A Face like my face that receives thee ; a Man like to
    me,
Thou shalt love and be loved by, for ever : a Hand
    like this hand
Shall throw open the gates of new life to thee ! See
    the Christ stand ! "

XIX

I know not too well how I found my way home in the
    night.
There were witnesses, cohorts about me, to left and to
    right,
Angels, powers, the unuttered, unseen, the alive, the
    aware :
I repressed, I got through them as hardly, as strug-
    glingly there,
As a runner beset by the populace famished for news—
Life or death. The whole earth was awakened, hell
    loosed with her crews ;
And the stars of night beat with emotion, and tingled
    and shot
Out in fire the strong pain of pent knowledge : but I
    fainted not,
For the Hand still impelled me at once and supported,
    suppressed
All the tumult, and quenched it with quiet, and holy
    behest,

Till the rapture was shut in itself, and the earth sank
    to rest.

Anon at the dawn, all that trouble had withered from
    earth—

Not so much, but I saw it die out in the day's tender
    birth ;

In the gathered intensity brought to the grey of the
    hills ;

In the shuddering forests' held breath ; in the sudden
    wind-thrills ;

In the startled wild beasts that bore off, each with eye
    sidling still

Though averted with wonder and dread ; in the birds
    stiff and chill

That rose heavily, as I approached them, made stupid
    with awe :

E'en the serpent that slid away silent,—he felt the new
    law.

The same stared in the white humid faces upturned by
    the flowers ;

The same worked in the heart of the cedar and moved
    the vine-bowers :

And the little brooks witnessing murmured, persistent
    and low,

With their obstinate, all but hushed voices—" E'en
    so, it is so ! "

ROBERT BROWNING.

MORTE D'ARTHUR

(EXTRACT.)

[King Arthur, from the barge of the three Queens,
which is to carry him to his rest, bids farewell to Sir
Bedivere, his last faithful knight.]

THEN loudly cried the bold Sir Bedivere :
  " Ah ! my Lord Arthur, whither shall I go ?

Where shall I hide my forehead and my eyes ?
For now I see the true old times are dead,
When every morning brought a noble chance,
And every chance brought out a noble knight.
Such times have been not since the light that led
The holy Elders with the gift of myrrh.
But now the whole ROUND TABLE is dissolved
Which was an image of the mighty world ;
And I, the last, go forth companionless,
And the days darken round me, and the years,
Among new men, strange faces, other minds."

    And slowly answer'd Arthur from the barge :
" The old order changeth, yielding place to new,
And God fulfils Himself in many ways,
Lest one good custom should corrupt the world.
Comfort thyself : what comfort is in me ?
I have lived my life, and that which I have done
May He within Himself make pure ! but thou,
If thou shouldst never see my face again,
Pray for my soul.   More things are wrought by prayer
Than this world dreams of.   Wherefore, let thy voice
Rise like a fountain for me night and day.
For what are men better than sheep or goats
That nourish a blind life within the brain,
If, knowing God, they lift not hands of prayer
Both for themselves and those who call them friend ?
For so the whole round earth is every way
Bound by gold chains about the feet of God.
But now farewell.   I am going a long way
With these thou seëst—if indeed I go—
(For all my mind is clouded with a doubt)
To the island-valley of Avilion ;
Where falls not hail, or rain, or any snow,
Nor ever wind blows loudly ; but it lies
Deep-meadow'd, happy, fair with orchard-lawns
And bowery hollows crown'd with summer sea,
Where I will heal me of my grievous wound."

                              LORD TENNYSON.

CONFESSIONS

WHAT is he buzzing in my ears ?
   " Now that I come to die,
Do I view the world as a vale of tears ? "
   Ah, reverend sir, not I !

What I viewed there once, what I view again
   Where the physic bottles stand
On the table's edge,—is a suburb lane,
   With a wall to my bedside hand.

That lane sloped, much as the bottles do,
   From a house you could descry
O'er the garden-wall : is the curtain blue
   Or green to a healthy eye ?

To mine, it serves for the old June weather
   Blue above lane and wall ;
And that farthest bottle labelled " Ether "
   Is the house o'er-topping all.

At a terrace, somewhat near the stopper,
   There watched for me, one June,
A girl : I know, sir, it's improper,
   My poor mind's out of tune.

Only, there was a way . . . you crept
   Close by the side, to dodge
Eyes in the house, two eyes except :
   They styled their house " The Lodge."

What right had a lounger up their lane ?
   But, by creeping very close,
With the good wall's help,—their eyes might strain
   And stretch themselves to Oes,

Yet never catch her and me together,
    As she left the attic, there,
By the rim of the bottle labelled " Ether,"
    And stole from stair to stair,

And stood by the rose-wreathed gate.   Alas,
    We loved, sir—used to meet :
How sad and bad and mad it was—
    But then, how it was sweet !

ROBERT BROWNING.

THE MAY QUEEN

You must wake and call me early, call me early,
    mother dear :
To-morrow 'ill be the happiest time of all the glad
    New-year ;
Of all the glad New-year, mother, the maddest merriest
    day ;
For I'm to be Queen o' the May, mother, I'm to be
    Queen o' the May.

There's many a black, black eye, they say, but none
    so bright as mine ;
There's Margaret and Mary, there's Kate and Caroline :
But none so fair as little Alice in all the land, they say ;
So I'm to be Queen o' the May, mother, I'm to be
    Queen o' the May.

I sleep so sound all night, mother, that I shall never
    wake,
If you do not call me loud when the day begins to
    break :
But I must gather knots of flowers, and buds and
    garlands gay,
For I'm to be Queen o' the May, mother, I'm to be
    Queen o' the May.

As I came up the valley whom think ye should I see,
But Robin leaning on the bridge beneath the hazel-
    tree ?
He thought of that sharp look, mother, I gave him
    yesterday,—
But I'm to be Queen o' the May, mother, I'm to be
    Queen o' the May.

He thought I was a ghost, mother, for I was all in
    white,
And I ran by him without speaking, like a flash of
    light.
They call me cruel-hearted, but I care not what they
    say,
For I'm to be Queen o' the May, mother, I'm to be
    Queen o' the May.

They say he's dying all for love, but that can never be :
They say his heart is breaking, mother—what is that
    to me ?
There's many a bolder lad 'ill woo me any summer day,
And I'm to be Queen o' the May, mother, I'm to be
    Queen o' the May.

Little Effie shall go with me to-morrow to the green,
And you'll be there, too, mother, to see me made the
    Queen ;
For the shepherd lads on every side 'ill come from far
    away,
And I'm to be Queen o' the May, mother, I'm to be
    Queen o' the May.

The honeysuckle round the porch has wov'n its wavy
    bowers,
And by the meadow-trenches blow the faint sweet
    cuckoo-flowers ;

(2,599)

14

And the wild marsh-marigold shines like fire in
 swamps and hollows grey,
And I'm to be Queen o' the May, mother, I'm to be
 Queen o' the May.

The night-winds come and go, mother, upon the
 meadow-grass,
And the happy stars above them seem to brighten as
 they pass ;
There will not be a drop of rain the whole of the live-
 long day,
And I'm to be Queen o' the May, mother, I'm to be
 Queen o' the May.

All the valley, mother, 'ill be fresh and green and still,
And the cowslip and the crowfoot are over all the hill,
And the rivulet in the flowery dale 'ill merrily glance
 and play,
For I'm to be Queen o' the May, mother, I'm to be
 Queen o' the May.

So you must wake and call me early, call me early,
 mother dear,
To-morrow 'ill be the happiest time of all the glad
 New-year :
To-morrow 'ill be of all the year the maddest merriest
 day,
For I'm to be Queen o' the May, mother, I'm to be
 Queen o' the May.

NEW-YEAR'S EVE

If you're waking call me early, call me early, mother
 dear,
For I would see the sun rise upon the glad New-year.
It is the last New-year that I shall ever see,
Then you may lay me low i' the mould, and think no
 more of me.

To-night I saw the sun set : he set and left behind
The good old year, the dear old time, and all my peace
    of mind ;
And the New-year's coming up, mother, but I shall
    never see
The blossom on the blackthorn, the leaf upon the tree.

Last May we made a crown of flowers : we had a merry
    day ;
Beneath the hawthorn on the green they made me
    Queen of May ;
And we danced about the maypole and in the hazel
    copse,
Till Charles's Wain came out above the tall white
    chimney-tops.

There's not a flower on all the hills : the frost is on the
    pane :
I only wish to live till the snowdrops come again :
I wish the snow would melt and the sun come out on
    high :
I long to see a flower so before the day I die.

The building rook 'ill caw from the windy tall elm-tree,
And the tufted plover pipe along the fallow lea,
And the swallow 'ill come back again with summer o'er
    the wave,
But I shall lie alone, mother, within the mouldering
    grave.

Upon the chancel-casement, and upon that grave of
    mine,
In the early early morning the summer sun 'ill shine,
Before the red cock crows from the farm upon the hill,
When you are warm asleep, mother, and all the world
    is still.

When the flowers come again, mother, beneath the
    waning light
You'll never see me more in the long grey fields at
    night ;
When from the dry dark wold the summer airs blow
    cool
On the oat-grass and the sword-grass, and the bulrush
    in the pool.

You'll bury me, my mother, just beneath the haw-
    thorn shade,
And you'll come sometimes and see me where I am
    lowly laid.
I shall not forget you, mother, I shall hear you when
    you pass,
With your feet above my head in the long and pleasant
    grass.

I have been wild and wayward, but you'll forgive me
    now :
You'll kiss me, my own mother, and forgive me ere
    I go ;—
Nay, nay, you must not weep, nor let your grief be
    wild,
You should not fret for me, mother, you have another
    child.

If I can I'll come again, mother, from out my resting-
    place :
Though you'll not see me, mother, I shall look upon
    your face ;
Though I cannot speak a word, I shall harken what
    you say,
And be often, often with you when you think I'm
    far away.

Good-night, good-night ! when I have said good-night
    for evermore,

And you see me carried out from the threshold of the
   door,
Don't let Effie come to see me till my grave be growing
   green :
She'll be a better child to you than ever I have been.

She'll find my garden-tools upon the granary floor :
Let her take 'em : they are hers : I shall never garden
   more :
But tell her, when I'm gone, to train the rose-bush
   that I set
About the parlour-window and the box of mignonette.

Good-night, sweet mother : call me before the day is
   born.
All night I lie awake, but I fall asleep at morn ;
But I would see the sun rise upon the glad New-year,
So, if you're waking, call me, call me early, mother
   dear.

CONCLUSION

I thought to pass away before, and yet alive I am ;
And in the fields all round I hear the bleating of the
   lamb.
How sadly, I remember, rose the morning of the year !
To die before the snowdrop came, and now the violet's
   here.

O sweet is the new violet, that comes beneath the skies,
And sweeter is the young lamb's voice to me that can-
   not rise,
And sweet is all the land about, and all the flowers that
   blow,
And sweeter far is death than life to me that long to go.

It seem'd so hard at first, mother, to leave the blessed
   sun ;

And now it seems as hard to stay, and yet His will be
 done !
But still I think it can't be long before I find release ;
And that good man, the clergyman, has told me words
 of peace.

O blessings on his kindly voice and on his silver hair !
And blessings on his whole life long, until he meet me
 there !
O blessings on his kindly heart and on his silver head !
A thousand times I blest him, as he knelt beside my
 bed.

He taught me all the mercy, for he show'd me all the
 sin.
Now, though my lamp was lighted late, there's One
 will let me in.
Nor would I now be well, mother, again, if that
 could be,
For my desire is but to pass to Him that died for me.

I did not hear the dog howl, mother, or the death-
 watch beat,
There came a sweeter token when the night and morning meet :
But sit beside my bed, mother, and put your hand in
 mine,
And Effie on the other side, and I will tell the sign.

All in the wild March-morning I heard the angels call ;
It was when the moon was setting, and the dark was
 over all ;
The trees began to whisper, and the wind began to roll,
And in the wild March-morning I heard them call
 my soul.

For lying broad awake I thought of you and Effie
 dear ;
I saw you sitting in the house, and I no longer here ;

With all my strength I pray'd for both, and so I felt
 resign'd,
And up the valley came a swell of music on the wind.

I thought that it was fancy, and I listen'd in my bed,
And then did something speak to me—I know not
 what was said ;
For great delight and shuddering took hold of all my
 mind,
And up the valley came again the music on the wind.

But you were sleeping ; and I said, " It's not for them :
 it's mine."
And if it comes three times, I thought, I take it for
 a sign.
And once again it came, and close beside the window-
 bars,
Then seem'd to go right up to Heaven and die among
 the stars.

So now I think my time is near. I trust it is. I know
The blessed music went that way my soul will have
 to go.
And for myself, indeed, I care not if I go to-day.
But, Effie, you must comfort *her* when I am pass'd
 away.

And say to Robin a kind word, and tell him not to fret;
There's many worthier than I, would make him happy
 yet.
If I had lived—I cannot tell—I might have been his
 wife ;
But all these things have ceased to be, with my desire
 of life.

O look ! the sun begins to rise, the heavens are in a
 glow ;
He shines upon a hundred fields, and all of them I
 know.

And there I move no longer now, and there his light
    may shine—
Wild flowers in the valley for other hands than mine.

O sweet and strange it seems to me, that ere this day
    is done
The voice that now is speaking may be beyond the
    sun—
For ever and for ever with those just souls and true—
And what is life, that we should moan ? why make we
    such ado ?

For ever and for ever, all in a blessed home—
And there to wait a little while, till you and Effie
    come—
To lie within the light of God, as I lie upon your
    breast—
And the wicked cease from troubling, and the weary
    are at rest.

Lord Tennyson.

BISHOP BLOUGRAM'S APOLOGY

(extract.)

[Bishop Blougram, a *bon vivant*, and a typical
Renaissance prince of the Church, is suspected of in-
sincerity by Mr. Gigadibs, a smart young man of letters.
After dinner the Bishop good-humouredly defends his
theological position.]

So, you despise me, Mr. Gigadibs,
No deprecation,—nay, I beg you, sir !
Beside 'tis our engagement : don't you know,
I promised, if you'd watch a dinner out,
We'd see truth dawn together ?—truth that peeps
Over the glass's edge when dinner's done,
And body gets its sop and holds its noise

And leaves soul free a little. Now's the time :
'Tis break of day ! You do despise me then.
And if I say, " despise me,"—never fear !
I know you do not in a certain sense—
Not in my arm-chair, for example : here,
I well imagine you respect my place
(*Status*, *entourage*, worldly circumstance)
Quite to its value—very much indeed :
—Are up to the protesting eyes of you
In pride at being seated here for once—
You'll turn it to such capital account !
When somebody, through years and years to come,
Hints of the bishop,—names me—that's enough :
" Blougram ? I knew him "—(into it you slide)
" Dined with him once, a Corpus Christi Day,
All alone, we two ; he's a clever man :
And after dinner,—why, the wine you know,—
Oh, there was wine, and good !—what with the wine . . .
'Faith, we began upon all sorts of talk !
He's no bad fellow, Blougram ; he had seen
Something of mine he relished, some review :
He's quite above their humbug in his heart,
Half-said as much, indeed—the thing's his trade.
I warrant, Blougram's sceptical at times :
How otherwise ? I liked him, I confess ! "
Che, che, my dear sir, as we say at Rome,
Don't you protest now ! It's fair give and take ;
You have had your turn and spoken your home-
    truths :
The hand's mine now, and here you follow suit.

    Thus much conceded, still the first fact stays—
You do despise me ; your ideal of life
Is not the bishop's : you would not be I.
You would like better to be Goethe, now,
Or Buonaparte, or, bless me, lower still,
Count D'Orsay,—so you did what you preferred,
Spoke as you thought, and, as you cannot help,

Believed or disbelieved, no matter what,
So long as on that point, whate'er it was,
You loosed your mind, were whole and sole yourself.
—That, my ideal never can include,
Upon that element of truth and worth
Never be based ! for say they make me Pope
(They can't—suppose it for our argument)
Why, there I'm at my tether's end, I've reached
My height, and not a height which pleases you :
An unbelieving Pope won't do, you say.
It's like those eerie stories nurses tell,
Of how some actor played Death on a stage,
With pasteboard crown, sham orb and tinselled dart,
And called himself the monarch of the world ;
Then, going in the tire-room afterward,
Because the play was done, to shift himself,
Got touched upon the sleeve familiarly,
The moment he had shut the closet door,
By Death himself.   Thus God might touch a Pope
At unawares, ask what his baubles mean,
And whose part he presumed to play just now ?
Best be yourself, imperial, plain and true !

So, drawing comfortable breath again,
You weigh and find, whatever more or less
I boast of my ideal realized,
Is nothing in the balance when opposed
To your ideal, your grand simple life,
Of which you will not realize one jot.
I am much, you are nothing ; you would be all,
I would be merely much : you beat me there.

No, friend, you do not beat me : hearken why.
The common problem, yours, mine, every one's,
Is—not to fancy what were fair in life
Provided it could be,—but, finding first
What may be, then find how to make it fair
Up to our means : a very different thing !

No abstract intellectual plan of life
Quite irrespective of life's plainest laws,
But one, a man, who is man and nothing more,
May lead within a world which (by your leave)
Is Rome or London, not Fool's-paradise.
Embellish Rome, idealize away,
Make paradise of London if you can,
You're welcome, nay, you're wise.

A simile !

We mortals cross the ocean of this world
Each in his average cabin of a life ;
The best's not big, the worst yields elbow-room.
Now for our six months' voyage—how prepare ?
You come on shipboard with a landsman's list
Of things he calls convenient : so they are !
An India screen is pretty furniture,
A piano-forte is a fine resource,
All Balzac's novels occupy one shelf,
The new edition fifty volumes long ;
And little Greek books, with the funny type
They get up well at Leipsic, fill the next :
Go on ! slabbed marble, what a bath it makes !
And Parma's pride, the Jerome, let us add !
'Twere pleasant could Correggio's fleeting glow
Hang full in face of one where'er one roams,
Since he more than the others brings with him
Italy's self,—the marvellous Modenese !
Yet was not on your list before, perhaps.
—Alas, friend, here's the agent . . . is't the name ?
The captain, or whoever's master here—
You see him screw his face up ; what's his cry
Ere you set foot on shipboard ?   " Six feet square ! "
If you won't understand what six feet mean,
Compute and purchase stores accordingly—
And if, in pique because he overhauls
Your Jerome, piano and bath, you come on board
Bare—why, you cut a figure at the first
While sympathetic landsmen see you off ;

Not afterward, when long ere half seas over,
You peep up from your utterly naked boards
Into some snug and well-appointed berth,
Like mine for instance (try the cooler jug—
Put back the other, but don't jog the ice !)
And mortified you mutter " Well and good ;
He sits enjoying his sea-furniture ;
'Tis stout and proper, and there's store of it :
Though I've the better notion, all agree,
Of fitting rooms up.   Hang the carpenter,
Neat ship-shape fixings and contrivances—
I would have brought my Jerome, frame and all ! "
And meantime you bring nothing : never mind—
You've proved your artist-nature : what you don't
You might bring, so despise me, as I say.

Now come, let's backward to the starting-place.
See my way : we're two college friends, suppose.
Prepare together for our voyage, then ;
Each note and check the other in his work,—
Here's mine, a bishop's outfit ; criticize !
What's wrong ? why won't you be a bishop too ?

Why first, you don't believe, you don't and can't,
(Not stately, that is, and fixedly
And absolutely and exclusively)
In any revelation called divine.
No dogmas nail your faith ; and what remains
But say so, like the honest man you are ?
First, therefore, overhaul theology !
Nay, I too, not a fool, you please to think,
Must find believing every whit as hard :
And if I do not frankly say as much,
The ugly consequence is clear enough.

Now wait, my friend : well, I do not believe—
If you'll accept no faith that is not fixed,
Absolute and exclusive, as you say,

You're wrong—I mean to prove it in due time.
Meanwhile, I know where difficulties lie
I could not, cannot solve, nor ever shall,
So give up hope accordingly to solve—
(To you, and over the wine). Our dogmas then
With both of us, though in unlike degree,
Missing full credence—overboard with them !
I mean to meet you on your own premise :
Good, there go mine in company with yours !

    And now what are we ? unbelievers both,
Calm and complete, determinately fixed
To-day, to-morrow and for ever, pray ?
You'll guarantee me that ? Not so, I think !
In no wise ! all we've gained is, that belief,
As unbelief before, shakes us by fits,
Confounds us like its predecessor. Where's
The gain ? how can we guard our unbelief,
Make it bear fruit to us ?—the problem here.
Just when we are safest, there's a sunset-touch,
A fancy from a flower-bell, some one's death,
A chorus-ending from Euripides,—
And that's enough for fifty hopes and fears
As old and new at once as nature's self,
To rap and knock and enter in our soul,
Take hands and dance there, a fantastic ring,
Round the ancient idol, on his base again,—
The grand Perhaps ! We look on helplessly.
There the old misgivings, crooked questions are—
This good God,—what he could do, if he would,
Would, if he could—then must have done long since :
If so, when, where and how ? some way must be,—
Once feel about, and soon or late you hit
Some sense, in which it might be, after all.
Why not, " The Way, the Truth, the Life ? "

                           —That way
Over the mountain, which who stands upon

Is apt to doubt if it be indeed a road ;
While if he view it from the waste itself,
Up goes the line there, plain from base to brow,
Not vague, mistakeable ! what's a break or two
Seen from the unbroken desert either side ?
And then (to bring in fresh philosophy)
What if the breaks themselves should prove at last
The most consummate of contrivances
To train a man's eye, teach him what is faith ?
And so we stumble at truth's very test !
All we have gained then by our unbelief
Is a life of doubt diversified by faith,
For one of faith diversified by doubt :
We called the chess-board white,—we call it black.

" Well," you rejoin, " the end's no worse, at least ;
We've reason for both colours on the board :
Why not confess then, where I drop the faith
And you the doubt, that I'm as right as you ? "

Because, friend, in the next place, this being so,
And both things even,—faith and unbelief
Left to a man's choice—we'll proceed a step,
Returning to our image, which I like.

A man's choice, yes—but a cabin-passenger's—
The man made for the special life of the world—
Do you forget him ? I remember though !
Consult our ship's conditions and you find
One and but one choice suitable to all ;
The choice, that you unluckily prefer,
Turning things topsy-turvy—they or it
Going to the ground. Belief or unbelief
Bears upon life, determines its whole course,
Begins at its beginning. See the world
Such as it is,—you made it not, nor I ;
I mean to take it as it is,—and you
Not so you'll take it,—though you get nought else.

I know the special kind of life I like,
What suits the most my idiosyncrasy,
Brings out the best of me and bears me fruit
In power, peace, pleasantness and length of days.
I find that positive belief does this
For me, and unbelief, no whit of this.
—For you, it does, however ?—that, we'll try !
'Tis clear, I cannot lead my life, at least,
Induce the world to let me peaceably,
Without declaring at the outset, " Friends,
I absolutely and peremptorily
Believe ! "—I say, faith is my waking life :
One sleeps, indeed, and dreams at intervals,
We know, but waking's the main point with us,
And my provision's for life's waking part.
Accordingly, I use heart, head and hand
All day, I build, scheme, study, and make friends ;
And when night overtakes me, down I lie,
Sleep, dream a little, and get done with it,
The sooner the better, to begin afresh.
What's midnight doubt before the dayspring's faith ?
You, the philosopher, that disbelieve,
That recognize the night, give dreams their weight—
To be consistent you should keep your bed,
Abstain from healthy acts that prove you man,
For fear you drowse perhaps at unawares !
And certainly at night you'll sleep and dream,
Live through the day and bustle as you please.
And so you live to sleep as I to wake,
To unbelieve as I to still believe ?
Well, and the common sense of the world calls you
Bed-ridden,—and its good things come to me.
Its estimation, which is half the fight,
That's the first-cabin comfort I secure :
The next ... but you perceive with half an eye !
Come, come, it's best believing, if we may ;
You can't but own that !

ROBERT BROWNING.

ABT VOGLER

(AFTER HE HAS BEEN EXTEMPORIZING UPON THE MUSICAL INSTRUMENT OF HIS INVENTION)

I

WOULD that the structure brave, the manifold music I
build,
Bidding my organ obey, calling its keys to their
work,
Claiming each slave of the sound, at a touch, as when
Solomon willed
Armies of angels that soar, legions of demons that
lurk,
Man, brute, reptile, fly,—alien of end and of aim,
Adverse, each from the other heaven-high, hell-deep
removed,—
Should rush into sight at once as he named the inef-
fable Name,
And pile him a palace straight, to pleasure the
princess he loved !

II

Would it might tarry like his, the beautiful building of
mine,
This which my keys in a crowd pressed and im-
portuned to raise !
Ah, one and all, how they helped, would dispart now
and now combine,
Zealous to hasten the work, heighten their master
his praise !
And one would bury his brow with a blind plunge
down to hell,
Burrow awhile and build, broad on the roots of
things,

Then up again swim into sight, having based me my
  palace well,
  Founded it, fearless of flame, flat on the nether
  springs.

III

And another would mount and march, like the ex-
  cellent minion he was,
  Ay, another and yet another, one crowd but with
  many a crest,
Raising my rampired walls of gold as transparent as
  glass,
  Eager to do and die, yield each his place to the rest :
For higher still and higher (as a runner tips with fire,
  When a great illumination surprises a festal night —
Outlining round and round Rome's dome from space
  to spire)
  Up, the pinnacled glory reached, and the pride of
  my soul was in sight.

IV

In sight ? Not half ! for it seemed, it was certain, to
  match man's birth,
  Nature in turn conceived, obeying an impulse as I ;
And the emulous heaven yearned down, made effort to
  reach the earth,
  As the earth had done her best, in my passion, to
  scale the sky :
Novel splendours burst forth, grew familiar and dwelt
  with mine,
  Not a point nor peak but found and fixed its wandering star ;
Meteor-moons, balls of blaze : and they did not pale
  nor pine,
  For earth had attained to heaven, there was no
  more near nor far.

V

Nay more ; for there wanted not who walked in the
glare and glow,
  Presences plain in the place ; or, fresh from the
  Protoplast,
Furnished for ages to come, when a kindlier wind
should blow,
  Lured now to begin and live, in a house to their
  liking at last ;
Or else the wonderful Dead who have passed through
the body and gone,
  But were back once more to breathe in an old world
  worth their new :
What never had been, was now ; what was, as it shall
be anon ;
  And what is,—shall I say, matched both ? for I was
  made perfect too.

VI

All through my keys that gave their sounds to a wish
of my soul,
  All through my soul that praised as its wish flowed
  visibly forth,
All through music and me ! For think, had I painted
the whole,
  Why, there it had stood, to see, nor the process so
  wonder-worth :
Had I written the same, made verse—still, effect pro-
ceeds from cause,
  Ye know why the forms are fair, ye hear how the
  tale is told ;
It is all triumphant art, but art in obedience to
laws,
  Painter and poet are proud in the artist-list en-
  rolled :—

VII

But here is the finger of God, a flash of the will that
    can,
  Existent behind all laws, that made them and, lo,
    they are !
And I know not if, save in this, such gift be allowed to
    man,
  That out of three sounds he frame, not a fourth
    sound, but a star.
Consider it well : each tone of our scale in itself is
    nought ;
  It is everywhere in the world—loud, soft, and all is
    said :
Give it to me to use ! I mix it with two in my thought
  And, there ! Ye have heard and seen : consider
    and bow the head !

VIII

Well, it is gone at last, the palace of music I reared ;
  Gone ! and the good tears start, the praises that
    come too slow ;
For one is assured at first, one scarce can say that he
    feared,
  That he even gave it a thought, the gone thing was
    to go.
Never to be again ! But many more of the kind
  As good, nay, better perchance : is this your com-
    fort to me ?
To me, who must be saved because I cling with my
    mind
  To the same, same self, same love, same God : ay,
    what was, shall be.

IX

Therefore to whom turn I but to thee, the ineffable
    Name ?

Builder and maker, thou, of houses not made with
   hands !
What, have fear of change from thee who art ever the
   same ?
   Doubt that Thy power can fill the heart that Thy
      power expands ?
There shall never be one lost good ! What was, shall
   live as before ;
   The evil is null, is nought, is silence implying sound ;
What was good, shall be good, with, for evil, so much
      good more ;
   On the earth the broken arcs ; in the heaven, a
      perfect round.

X

All we have willed or hoped or dreamed of good, shall
   exist ;
   Not its semblance, but itself ; no beauty, nor good,
      nor power
Whose voice has gone forth, but each survives for the
   melodist
When eternity affirms the conception of an hour.
The high that proved too high, the heroic for earth
   too hard,
   The passion that left the ground to lose itself in the
      sky,
Are music sent up to God by the lover and the bard ;
   Enough that he heard it once : we shall hear it by-
      and-by.

XI

And what is our failure here but a triumph's evidence
   For the fulness of the days ? Have we withered or
      agonized ?
Why else was the pause prolonged but that singing
   might issue thence ?
   Why rushed the discords in, but that harmony
      should be prized ?

Sorrow is hard to bear, and doubt is slow to clear,
  Each sufferer says his say, his scheme of the weal
    and woe :
But God has a few of us whom he whispers in the ear ;
  The rest may reason and welcome : 'tis we
    musicians know.

XII

Well, it is earth with me ; silence resumes her reign :
  I will be patient and proud, and soberly acquiesce.
Give me the keys. I feel for the common chord again,
  Sliding by semitones, till I sink to the minor,—yes,
And I blunt it into a ninth, and I stand on alien
    ground,
  Surveying awhile the heights I rolled from into the
    deep ;
Which, hark, I have dared and done, for my resting-
    place is found,
  The C Major of this life : so, now I will try to sleep.
                                ROBERT BROWNING.

RABBI BEN EZRA

Grow old along with me !
The best is yet to be,
The last of life, for which the first was made :
Our times are in His hand
Who saith " A whole I planned,
Youth shows but half ; trust God : see all, nor be
    afraid ! "

Not that, amassing flowers,
Youth sighed " Which rose make ours,
Which lily leave and then as best recall ? "

Not that, admiring stars,
It yearned " Nor Jove, nor Mars ;
Mine be some figured flame which blends, transcends
    them all ! "

Not for such hopes and fears
Annulling youth's brief years,
Do I remonstrate : folly wide the mark !
Rather I prize the doubt
Low kinds exist without,
Finished and finite clods, untroubled by a spark.

Poor vaunt of life indeed,
Were man but formed to feed
On joy, to solely seek and find and feast :
Such feasting ended, then
As sure an end to men ;
Irks care the crop-full bird ? Frets doubt the maw-
    crammed beast ?

Rejoice we are allied
To That which doth provide
And not partake, effect and not receive !
A spark disturbs our clod ;
Nearer we hold of God
Who gives, than of His tribes that take, I must believe.

Then, welcome each rebuff
That turns earth's smoothness rough,
Each sting that bids nor sit nor stand but go !
Be our joys three-parts pain !
Strive, and hold cheap the strain ;
Learn, nor account the pang ; dare, never grudge the
    throe !

For thence,—a paradox
Which comforts while it mocks,—
Shall life succeed in that it seems to fail :

What I aspired to be,
And was not, comforts me :
A brute I might have been, but would not sink i' the
    scale.

What is he but a brute
Whose flesh hath soul to suit,
Whose spirit works lest arms and legs want play ?
To man, propose this test—
Thy body at its best,
How far can that project thy soul on its lone way ?

Yet gifts should prove their use :
I own the Past profuse
Of power each side, perfection every turn :
Eyes, ears took in their dole,
Brain treasured up the whole ;
Should not the heart beat once " How good to live and
    learn ? "

Not once beat " Praise be Thine !
I see the whole design,
I, who saw power, see now Love perfect too :
Perfect I call Thy plan :
Thanks that I was a man !
Maker, remake, complete,—I trust what Thou shalt
    do ! "

For pleasant is this flesh ;
Our soul, in its rose-mesh
Pulled ever to the earth, still yearns for rest ;
Would we some prize might hold
To match those manifold
Possessions of the brute,—gain most, as we did best !

Let us not always say
" Spite of this flesh to-day
I strove, made head, gained ground upon the whole ! "

As the bird wings and sings,
Let us cry " All good things
Are ours, nor soul helps flesh more, now, than flesh
    helps soul ! ' "

Therefore I summon age
To grant youth's heritage,
Life's struggle having so far reached its term :
Thence shall I pass, approved
A man, for aye removed
From the developed brute ; a God though in the germ.

And I shall thereupon
Take rest, ere I be gone,
Once more on my adventure brave and new :
Fearless and unperplexed,
When I wage battle next,
What weapons to select, what armour to indue.

Youth ended, I shall try
My gain or loss thereby ;
Leave the fire ashes, what survives is gold :
And I shall weigh the same,
Give life its praise or blame :
Young, all lay in dispute ; I shall know, being old.

For note, when evening shuts,
A certain moment cuts
The dead off, calls the glory from the grey :
A whisper from the west
Shoots—" Add this to the rest,
Take it and try its worth : here dies another day."

So, still within this life,
Though lifted o'er its strife,
Let me discern, compare, pronounce at last,
" This rage was right i' the main,
That acquiescence vain ;
The Future I may face now I have proved the Past."

For more is not reserved
To man, with soul just nerved
To act to-morrow what he learns to-day :
Here, work enough to watch
The Master work, and catch
Hints of the proper craft, tricks of the tool's true play.

As it was better, youth
Should strive, through acts uncouth,
Toward making, than repose on aught found made ;
So, better, age, exempt
From strife, should know, than tempt
Further. Thou waitedst age ; wait death nor be
  afraid !

Enough now, if the Right
And Good and Infinite
Be named here, as thou callest thy hand thine own,
With knowledge absolute,
Subject to no dispute,
From fools that crowded youth, nor let thee feel alone.

Be there, for once and all,
Severed great minds from small,
Announced to each his station in the Past !
Was I, the world arraigned,
Were they, my soul disdained,
Right ?   Let age speak the truth and give us peace
  at last !

Now, who shall arbitrate ?
Ten men love what I hate,
Shun what I follow, slight what I receive ;
Ten, who in ears and eyes
Match me : we all surmise,
They, this thing, and I, that : whom shall my soul
  believe ?

Not on the vulgar mass
Called " work," must sentence pass,
Things done, that took the eye and had the price ;
O'er which, from level stand,
The low world laid its hand,
Found straightway to its mind, could value in a trice :

But all, the world's coarse thumb
And finger failed to plumb,
So passed in making up the main account ;
All instincts immature,
All purposes unsure,
That weighed not as his work, yet swelled the man's
    amount :

Thoughts hardly to be packed
Into a narrow act,
Fancies that broke through language and escaped ;
All I could never be,
All, men ignored in me,
This, I was worth to God, whose wheel the pitcher
    shaped.

Ay, note that Potter's wheel,
That metaphor ! and feel
Why time spins fast, why passive lies our clay,—
Thou, to whom fools propound,
When the wine makes its round,
" Since life fleets, all is change ; the Past gone, seize
    to-day ! "

Fool !   All that is, at all,
Lasts ever, past recall ;
Earth changes, but thy soul and God stand sure :
What entered into thee,
That was, is, and shall be :
Time's wheel runs back or stops : Potter and clay
    endure.

He fixed thee mid this dance
Of plastic circumstance,
This Present, thou, forsooth, wouldst fain arrest :
Machinery just meant
To give thy soul its bent,
Try thee and turn thee forth, sufficiently impressed.

What though the earlier grooves
Which ran the laughing loves
Around thy base, no longer pause and press ?
What though, about thy rim,
Scull-things in order grim
Grow out, in graver mood, obey the sterner stress ?

Look not thou down but up !
To uses of a cup,
The festal board, lamp's flash and trumpet's peal,
The new wine's foaming flow,
The Master's lips a-glow !
Thou, heaven's consummate cup, what needst thou
    with earth's wheel ?

But I need, now as then,
Thee, God, who mouldest men ;
And since, not even while the whirl was worst,
Did I,—to the wheel of life
With shapes and colours rife
Bound dizzily,—mistake my end, to slake Thy thirst :

So, take and use Thy work !
Amend what flaws may lurk,
What strain o' the stuff, what warpings past the aim !
My times be in Thy hand !
Perfect the cup as planned !
Let age approve of youth, and death complete the
    same !

ROBERT BROWNING.

IN MEMORIAM

A. H. H.

OBIIT MDCCCXXXIII

(EXTRACTS.)

STRONG Son of God, immortal Love,
    Whom we, that have not seen thy face,
    By faith, and faith alone, embrace,
Believing where we cannot prove ;

Thine are these orbs of light and shade ;
    Thou madest Life in man and brute ;
    Thou madest Death ; and lo, thy foot
Is on the skull which thou hast made.

Thou wilt not leave us in the dust :
    Thou madest man, he knows not why ;
    He thinks he was not made to die ;
And thou hast made him : thou art just.

Thou seemest human and divine,
    The highest, holiest manhood thou :
    Our wills are ours, we know not how ;
Our wills are ours, to make them thine.

Our little systems have their day ;
    They have their day, and cease to be ;
    They are but broken lights of thee,
And thou, O Lord, art more than they.

We have but faith : we cannot know ;
    For knowledge is of things we see ;
    And yet we trust it comes from thee,
A beam in darkness : let it grow.

Let knowledge grow from more to more,
    But more of reverence in us dwell ;
    That mind and soul, according well,
May make one music as before.

But vaster.   We are fools and slight ;
    We mock thee when we do not fear :
    But help thy foolish one to bear,
Help thy vain worlds to bear thy light.

Forgive what seem'd my sin in me,
    What seem'd my worth since I began ;
    For merit lives from man to man,
And not from man, O Lord, to thee.

Forgive my grief for one removed,
    Thy creature, whom I found so fair.
    I trust he lives in thee, and there
I find him worthier to be loved.

Forgive these wild and wandering cries,
    Confusions of a wasted youth ;
    Forgive them where they fail in truth,
And in thy wisdom make me wise.

I

I held it truth, with him who sings
    To one clear harp in divers tones,
    That men may rise on stepping-stones
Of their dead selves to higher things.

But who shall so forecast the years
    And find in loss a gain to match ?
    Or reach a hand through time to catch
The far-off interest of tears ?

Let Love clasp Grief lest both be drown'd,
    Let darkness keep her raven gloss ;
    Ah, sweeter to be drunk with loss,
To dance with death, to beat the ground,

Than that the victor Hours should scorn
    The long result of love, and boast :
    " Behold the man that loved and lost,
But all he was is overworn."

VI

One writes, that " Other friends remain,"
    That " Loss is common to the race "—
    And common is the commonplace,
And vacant chaff well meant for grain.

That loss is common could not make
    My own less bitter, rather more :
    Too common !   Never morning wore
To evening, but some heart did break.

O father, wheresoe'er thou be,
    That pledgest now thy gallant son ;
    A shot, ere half thy draught be done,
Hath still'd the life that beat from thee.

O mother, praying God will save
    Thy sailor,—while thy head is bow'd,
    His heavy-shotted hammock-shroud
Drops in his vast and wandering grave.

Ye know no more than I who wrought
    At that last hour to please him well ;
    Who mused on all I had to tell,
And something written, something thought ;

Expecting still his advent home ;
 And ever met him on his way
 With wishes, thinking, here to-day,
Or here to-morrow will he come.

O somewhere, meek, unconscious dove,
 That sittest ranging golden hair ;
 And glad to find thyself so fair,
Poor child, that waitest for thy love !

For now her father's chimney glows
 In expectation of a guest ;
 And thinking " This will please him best,"
She takes a riband or a rose ;

For he will see them on to-night :
 And with the thought her colour burns ;
 And, having left the glass, she turns
Once more to set a ringlet right ;

And, even when she turn'd, the curse
 Had fallen, and her future Lord
 Was drown'd in passing through the ford,
Or kill'd in falling from his horse.

Oh what to her shall be the end ?
 And what to me remains of good ?
 To her, perpetual maidenhood ;
And unto me, no second friend.

IX

Fair ship, that from the Italian shore,
 Sailest the placid ocean-plains
 With my lost Arthur's loved remains,
Spread thy full wings, and waft him o'er.

So draw him home to those that mourn
    In vain ; a favourable speed
    Ruffle thy mirror'd mast, and lead
Through prosperous floods his holy urn.

All night no ruder air perplex
    Thy sliding keel, till Phosphor, bright
    As our pure love, through early light
Shall glimmer on the dewy decks.

Sphere all your lights around, above ;
    Sleep, gentle heavens, before the prow ;
    Sleep, gentle winds, as he sleeps now,
My friend, the brother of my love ;

My Arthur, whom I shall not see
    Till all my widow'd race be run ;
    Dear as the mother to the son,
More than my brothers are to me.

X

I hear the noise about thy keel ;
    I hear the bell struck in the night ;
    I see the cabin-window bright ;
I see the sailor at the wheel.

Thou bring'st the sailor to his wife,
    And travell'd men from foreign lands ;
    And letters unto trembling hands ;
And, thy dark freight, a vanish'd life.

So bring him : we have idle dreams :
    This look of quiet flatters thus
    Our home-bred fancies : oh, to us,
The fools of habit, sweeter seems

To rest beneath the clover sod,
    That takes the sunshine and the rains,
    Or where the kneeling hamlet drains
The chalice of the grapes of God ;

Than if with thee the roaring wells
    Should gulf him fathom-deep in brine ;
    And hands so often clasp'd in mine,
Should toss with tangle and with shells.

XI

Calm is the morn without a sound,
    Calm as to suit a calmer grief,
    And only through the faded leaf
The chestnut pattering to the ground :

Calm and deep peace on this high wold,
    And on these dews that drench the furze,
    And all the silvery gossamers
That twinkle into green and gold :

Calm and still light on yon great plain
    That sweeps with all its autumn bowers,
    And crowded farms and lessening towers,
To mingle with the bounding main :

Calm and deep peace in this wide air,
    These leaves that redden to the fall ;
    And in my heart, if calm at all,
If any calm, a calm despair :

Calm on the seas, and silver sleep,
    And waves that sway themselves in rest,
    And dead calm in that noble breast
Which heaves but with the heaving deep.

XV

To-night the winds begin to rise
 And roar from yonder dropping day ;
 The last red leaf is whirl'd away,
The rooks are blown about the skies ;

The forest crack'd, the waters curl'd,
 The cattle huddled on the lea ;
 And wildly dash'd on tower and tree
The sunbeam strikes along the world :

And but for fancies, which aver
 That all thy motions gently pass
 Athwart a plane of molten glass,
I scarce could brook the strain and stir

That makes the barren branches loud ;
 And but for fear it is not so,
 The wild unrest that lives in woe
Would dote and pore on yonder cloud

That rises upward always higher,
 And onward drags a labouring breast,
 And topples round the dreary west,
A looming bastion fringed with fire.

XVII

Thou comest, much wept for : such a breeze
 Compell'd thy canvas, and my prayer
 Was as the whisper of an air
To breathe thee over lonely seas.

For I in spirit saw thee move
　　Through circles of the bounding sky ;
　　Week after week : the days go by :
Come quick, thou bringest all I love.

Henceforth, wherever thou mayst roam,
　　My blessing, like a line of light,
　　Is on the waters day and night,
And like a beacon guards thee home.

So may whatever tempest mars
　　Mid-ocean, spare thee, sacred bark ;
　　And balmy drops in summer dark
Slide from the bosom of the stars.

So kind an office hath been done,
　　Such precious relics brought by thee ;
　　The dust of him I shall not see
Till all my widow'd race be run.

XIX

The Danube to the Severn gave
　　The darken'd heart that beat no more ;
　　They laid him by the pleasant shore,
And in the hearing of the wave.

There twice a day the Severn fills ;
　　The salt sea-water passes by,
　　And hushes half the babbling Wye
And makes a silence in the hills.

The Wye is hush'd nor moved along ;
　　And hush'd my deepest grief of all,
　　When fill'd with tears that cannot fall,
I brim with sorrow drowning song.

The tide flows down, the wave again
    Is vocal in its wooded walls :
    My deeper anguish also falls,
And I can speak a little then.

XXXI

When Lazarus left his charnel-cave,
    And home to Mary's house return'd,
    Was this demanded—if he yearn'd
To hear her weeping by his grave ?

" Where wert thou, brother, those four days ? "
    There lives no record of reply,
    Which telling what it is to die
Had surely added praise to praise.

From every house the neighbours met,
    The streets were fill'd with joyful sound,
    A solemn gladness even crown'd
The purple brows of Olivet.

Behold a man raised up by Christ !
    The rest remaineth unreveal'd ;
    He told it not ; or something seal'd
The lips of that Evangelist.

XXXII

Her eyes are homes of silent prayer,
    Nor other thought her mind admits
    But, he was dead, and there he sits,
And he that brought him back is there.

Then one deep love doth supersede
    All other, when her ardent gaze
    Roves from the living brother's face,
And rests upon the Life indeed.

All subtle thought, all curious fears,
    Borne down by gladness so complete,
    She bows, she bathes the Saviour's feet
With costly spikenard and with tears.

Thrice blest whose lives are faithful prayers,
    Whose loves in higher love endure ;
    What souls possess themselves so pure,
Or is there blessedness like theirs ?

XXXIII

O thou that after toil and storm
    Mayst seem to have reach'd a purer air,
    Whose faith has centre everywhere,
Nor cares to fix itself to form,

Leave thou thy sister, when she prays,
    Her early Heaven, her happy views ;
    Nor thou with shadow'd hint confuse
A life that leads melodious days.

Her faith through form is pure as thine,
    Her hands are quicker unto good :
    Oh, sacred be the flesh and blood
To which she links a truth divine !

See thou, that countest reason ripe
    In holding by the law within,
    Thou fail not in a world of sin,
And ev'n for want of such a type.

XLIV

How fares it with the happy dead ?
    For here the man is more and more ;
    But he forgets the days before
God shut the doorways of his head.

The days have vanish'd, tone and tint,
    And yet perhaps the hoarding sense
    Gives out at times (he knows not whence)
A little flash, a mystic hint ;

And in the long harmonious years
    (If Death so taste Lethean springs)
    May some dim touch of earthly things
Surprise thee ranging with thy peers.

If such a dreamy touch should fall,
    O turn thee round, resolve the doubt ;
    My guardian angel will speak out
In that high place, and tell thee all.

LV

The wish, that of the living whole
    No life may fail beyond the grave,
    Derives it not from what we have
The likest God within the soul ?

Are God and Nature then at strife,
    That Nature lends such evil dreams ?
    So careful of the type she seems,
So careless of the single life ;

That I, considering everywhere
    Her secret meaning in her deeds,
    And finding that of fifty seeds
She often brings but one to bear,

I falter where I firmly trod,
    And falling with my weight of cares
    Upon the great world's altar-stairs
That slope through darkness up to God,

I stretch lame hands of faith, and grope,
>And gather dust and chaff, and call
>To what I feel is Lord of all,
And faintly trust the larger hope.

CVI

Ring out wild bells, to the wild sky,
>The flying cloud, the frosty light :
>The year is dying in the night ;
Ring out, wild bells, and let him die.

Ring out the old, ring in the new,
>Ring, happy bells, across the snow :
>The year is going, let him go ;
Ring out the false, ring in the true.

Ring out the grief that saps the mind,
>For those that here we see no more ;
>Ring out the feud of rich and poor,
Ring in redress to all mankind.

Ring out a slowly dying cause,
>And ancient forms of party strife ;
>Ring in the nobler modes of life,
With sweeter manners, purer laws.

Ring out the want, the care, the sin,
>The faithless coldness of the times ;
>Ring out, ring out my mournful rhymes,
But ring the fuller minstrel in.

Ring out false pride in place and blood,
>The civic slander and the spite ;
>Ring in the love of truth and right,
Ring in the common love of good.

Ring out old shapes of foul disease,
      Ring out the narrowing lust of gold ;
      Ring out the thousand wars of old,
Ring in the thousand years of peace.

Ring in the valiant man and free,
      The larger heart, the kindlier hand ;
      Ring out the darkness of the land,
Ring in the Christ that is to be.

CXV

Now fades the last long streak of snow,
      Now burgeons every maze of quick
      About the flowering squares, and thick
By ashen roots the violets blow.

Now rings the woodland loud and long,
      The distance takes a lovelier hue,
      And drown'd in yonder living blue
The lark becomes a sightless song.

Now dance the lights on lawn and lea,
      The flocks are whiter down the vale,
      And milkier every milky sail
On winding stream or distant sea ;

Where now the seamew pipes, or dives
      In yonder greening gleam, and fly
      The happy birds, that change their sky
To build and brood, that live their lives

From land to land : and in my breast
      Spring wakens too ; and my regret
      Becomes an April violet,
And buds and blossoms like the rest.

CXXVI

Love is and was my Lord and King,
    And in his presence I attend
    To hear the tidings of my friend,
Which every hour his couriers bring.

Love is and was my King and Lord,
    And will be, though as yet I keep
    Within his court on earth, and sleep
Encompass'd by his faithful guard,

And hear at times a sentinel
    That moves about from place to place
    And whispers to the vast of space
Among the worlds, that all is well.

CXXVII

And all is well, though faith and form
    Be sunder'd in the night of fear ;
    Well roars the storm to those that hear
A deeper voice across the storm,

Proclaiming social truth shall spread,
    And justice, ev'n though thrice again
    The red fool-fury of the Seine
Should pile her barricades with dead.

But ill for him that wears a crown,
    And him, the lazar, in his rags :
    They tremble, the sustaining crags ;
The spires of ice are toppled down,

And molten up, and roar in flood ;
    The fortress crashes from on high,
    The brute earth lightens to the sky,
And the great Æon sinks in blood,

And compass'd by the fires of hell,
    While thou, dear spirit, happy star,
    O'erlook'st the tumult from afar
And smilest, knowing all is well.

CXXVIII

The love that rose on stronger wings,
    Unpalsied when he met with Death,
    Is comrade of the lesser faith
That sees the course of human things.

No doubt vast eddies in the flood
    Of onward time shall yet be made,
    And thronèd races may degrade ;
Yet, O ye mysteries of good,

Wild Hours that fly with Hope and Fear,
    If all your office had to do
    With old results that look like new—
If this were all your mission here,

To draw, to sheathe a useless sword,
    To fool the crowd with glorious lies,
    To cleave a creed in sects and cries,
To change the bearing of a word,

To shift an arbitrary power,
    To cramp the student at his desk,
    To make old bareness picturesque
And tuft with grass a feudal tower ;

Why then my scorn might well descend
    On you and yours. I see in part
    That all, as in some piece of art,
Is toil coöperant to an end.

CXXIX

Dear friend, far off, my lost desire,
 So far, so near in woe and weal ;
 Oh, loved the most when most I feel
There is a lower and a higher ;

Known and unknown ; human, divine ;
 Sweet human hand and lips and eye ;
 Dear heavenly friend that canst not die,
Mine, mine, for ever, ever mine ;

Strange friend, past, present, and to be ;
 Loved deeplier, darklier understood ;
 Behold I dream a dream of good,
And mingle all the world with thee.

CXXX

Thy voice is on the rolling air ;
 I hear thee where the waters run ;
 Thou standest in the rising sun,
And in the setting thou art fair.

What art thou then ? I cannot guess ;
 But though I seem in star and flower
 To feel thee some diffusive power,
I do not therefore love thee less :

My love involves the love before ;
 My love is vaster passion now ;
 Though mix'd with God and Nature thou,
I seem to love thee more and more.

Far off thou art, but ever nigh ;
 I have thee still, and I rejoice ;
 I prosper, circled with thy voice ;
I shall not lose thee though I die.

CXXXI

O living will that shalt endure
    When all that seems shall suffer shock,
    Rise in the spiritual rock,
Flow through our deeds and make them pure,

That we may lift from out of dust
    A voice as unto him that hears,
    A cry above the conquer'd years
To one that with us works ; and trust,

With faith that comes of self-control,
    The truths that never can be proved
    Until we close with all we loved,
And all we flow from, soul in soul.

*   *   *   *   *   *   *

And rise, O moon, from yonder down,
    Till over down and over dale
    All night the shining vapour sail
And pass the silent-lighted town,

The white-faced halls, the glancing rills,
    And catch at every mountain head,
    And o'er the friths that branch and spread
Their sleeping silver through the hills ;

And touch with shade the bridal doors,
    With tender gloom the roof, the wall ;
    And breaking, let the splendour fall
To spangle all the happy shores

By which they rest, and ocean sounds,
    And, star and system rolling past,
    A soul shall draw from out the vast
And strike his being into bounds,

And, moved through life of lower phase,
    Result in man, be born and think,
    And act and love, a closer link
Betwixt us and the crowning race

Of those that, eye to eye, shall look
    On knowledge ; under whose command
    Is Earth and Earth's, and in their hand
Is Nature like an open book ;

No longer half-akin to brute,
    For all we thought, and loved, and did,
    And hoped, and suffer'd, is but seed
Of what in them is flower and fruit ;

Whereof the man, that with me trod
    This planet, was a noble type
    Appearing ere the times were ripe,
That friend of mine who lives in God—

That God, which ever lives and loves,
    One God, one law, one element,
    And one far-off divine event,
To which the whole creation moves.

LORD TENNYSON.

PROSPICE

FEAR death ?—to feel the fog in my throat,
  The mist in my face,
When the snows begin, and the blasts denote
  I am nearing the place,
The power of the night, the press of the storm,
  The post of the foe ;
Where he stands, the Arch Fear in a visible form,
  Yet the strong man must go :
For the journey is done and the summit attained,
  And the barriers fall,
Though a battle's to fight ere the guerdon be gained,
  The reward of it all.
I was ever a fighter, so—one fight more,
  The best and the last !
I would hate that death bandaged my eyes, and for-
    bore,
  And bade me creep past.
No ! let me taste the whole of it, fare like my peers
  The heroes of old,
Bear the brunt, in a minute pay glad life's arrears
  Of pain, darkness and cold.
For sudden the worst turns the best to the brave,
  The black minute's at end,
And the elements' rage, the fiend-voices that rave,
  Shall dwindle, shall blend,
Shall change, shall become first a peace out of pain,
  Then a light, then thy breast,
O thou soul of my soul ! I shall clasp thee again,
  And with God be the rest !

                                    ROBERT BROWNING.

PRINTED IN GREAT BRITAIN AT
THE PRESS OF THE PUBLISHERS

A Novel Poetic Anthology

THE TIDE OF TIME
In English Poetry

Edited by Sir Henry Newbolt

Being No. 24 of the " Teaching of English" Series

卍

¶ School Anthologies of Poetry are numerous, and
many are excellent. Teachers may reasonably ask
whether there is room for another.

¶ THE TIDE OF TIME is not merely an anthology
of modern and standard verse, but *a study of poetry*
by a recognized authority who is himself one of the
best of our modern poets.

¶ The study takes the form of an inquiry, which traces
the inspiration, material, and method of the modern
poets back to the earlier writers of verse. It is a
fascinating voyage up-stream to the sources, with
continual revelations of an interesting and sometimes
a surprising character.

¶ At the same time the book contains the best of English
poetry, from Chaucer to Bridges, and includes a large
amount of copyright material.